Breach of the Peace

Scottish Criminal Law and Practice Series

Series Editor

The Rt Hon The Lord McCluskey

Breach of the Peace

Michael G A Christie MA, LLB, Solicitor,
Lecturer in Private Law in the University of Aberdeen

Edinburgh
Butterworths
1990

United Kingdom	Butterworth & Co (Publishers) Ltd, 88 Kingsway, LONDON WC2B 6AB and 4 Hill Street, EDINBURGH EH2 3JZ
Australia	Butterworths Pty Ltd, SYDNEY, MELBOURNE, BRISBANE, ADELAIDE, PERTH, CANBERRA and HOBART
Canada	Butterworths Canada Ltd, TORONTO and VANCOUVER
Ireland	Butterworth (Ireland) Ltd, DUBLIN
Malaysia	Malayan Law Journal Sdn Bhd, KUALA LUMPUR
New Zealand	Butterworths of New Zealand Ltd, WELLINGTON and AUCKLAND
Puerto Rico	Equity de Puerto Rico, Inc, HATO REY
Singapore	Butterworth & Co (Asia) Pte Ltd, SINGAPORE
USA	Butterworth Legal Publishers, ST PAUL, Minnesota, SEATTLE, Washington, BOSTON, Massachusetts, AUSTIN, Texas and D & S Publishers, CLEARWATER, Florida

A CIP Catalogue record for this book is available from the British Library

ISBN 0 406 14430 3

Typeset, printed and bound by Thomson Litho Ltd, East Kilbride, Scotland

Preface

This short text explores the ambit of breach of the peace in Scots criminal law. Although this is an extremely common offence before district and sheriff courts, rather little has been written about it. An attempt has, therefore, been made to synthesise the relevant reported cases in a straightforward, non-jurisprudential way. It is hoped, no doubt with more optimism than can ultimately be justified, that this short exercise may help reveal the essential features of a crime famed abroad more for its obscurity than for its good sense.

Proper and grateful acknowledgment must be made here to Dr David C Coull, and to both Mrs Lorimer and Mrs Rae of his firm's secretarial staff. Their sterling efforts enabled the proofreading of the text to be undertaken during the autumn of 1989 when the author was teaching abroad at the Universities of Baltimore and Maryland. Proper and grateful acknowledgment is also due to the staff of Butterworths, for their indispensable and unfailing encouragement and support.

Michael G A Christie
December 1989

Contents

III CONDUCT AND RESULTS

APPENDIX

INDEX   109

Table of statutes

Table of cases

Abbreviations

Alison, Archibald: Principles of the Criminal Law of Scotland (1832)
                 Practice of the Criminal Law (1833)
Blackstone, William: Commentaries on the Laws of England (1765–1769)
Blair, William: The Scottish Justices' Manual (1834)
Burnett, John: Criminal Law of Scotland (1811)
Erskine, John: Institute of the Law of Scotland (1833 edn, by Nicolson, J B)
Hume, David: Commentaries on the Law of Scotland Respecting Crimes (1844 edn, by B R Bell)
Gane & Stoddart: A Casebook on Scottish Criminal Law (1988 edn, by Gane, C H W and Stoddart, C N)
Gordon, G H: Criminal Law (1978 edn; 1984 Supplement)
Hutcheson, Gilbert: Treatise of the Office of Justice of Peace (etc) (1809)
Macdonald, J H A: Criminal Law (1948 edn)
Mackenzie, Sir George: Laws & Customs of Scotland in Matters of Criminal (1678, 1699)
Nicholson, C G B: The Law & Practice of Sentencing in Scotland (1981; 1985 Supplement)
Renton & Brown: Criminal Procedure according to the Law of Scotland (5th edn, 1983, by G H Gordon)

I Introduction

A matter of common law

1.01 Breach of the peace is at basis a matter of common law. As such, its roots run deep. No authoritative case of whatever antiquity can, therefore, afford to be ignored, and no reported case concerned with breach of the peace is likely to be totally unhelpful. The common law, of course, develops and grows. Whilst examination of the root-structure yields abundant clues as to the likely development of a common law crime, it does not follow that its actual development must run true to some predetermined pattern. If there is merit in having a non-statutory, non-code-based system of criminal law, that merit surely lies in flexibility. Yet the standard criticism remains that breach of the peace was at one time a fixed and readily understood crime, fitting a clearly defined mould from which it, mutant like, escaped in modern times (see G H Gordon, *Crimes Without Laws?*, 1966 JR 214 at pp 216 and 225). It must be seriously doubted, however, whether such criticism can be justified. Breach of the peace seems always to have been loosely defined, and seems to have been rather a simple descriptor of a class of offences than a *nomen juris*.

Text writers as sources

1.02 In matters of the common law of Scotland, Hume's *Commentaries on the Law of Scotland Respecting Crimes* stands pre-eminent amongst text writers on the criminal law. Indeed, he is regarded as *the* source of the non-statutory law. Whilst it would be improper to think of his *Commentaries* as a fountain of principle, since he set out to write a practical work based on the records of the High Court of Justiciary (see vol I, Introduction, pp 13–14 and 18), it is still thought proper to accept the fruits of his researches in the Books of Adjournal without question. Although this may appear to be a surprising statement to any modern legal-historian schooled in more exacting research methods than could possibly have been known to an early nineteenth century Baron of Exchequer, the Scottish judiciary and legal professions have accepted the pre-eminence of *Hume* for so long a period of time that the matter can scarcely now be redargued. Any modern account of breach of the peace must, therefore, begin with Hume's account of the issue. (Amongst Hume's contemporaries, Burnett (*Criminal Law of Scotland* (1811)) has nothing, and Alison (*Principles of the Criminal Law of Scotland* (1832) and *Practice of the Criminal Law* (1833)) very little to contribute to any discussion of the present subject.)

Hume's views on breach of the peace

1.03   Hume arranged the order of crimes in volume I of his *Commentaries* under group headings. Thus, for example, chapters II to V (Theft, Reset, Wilful Fire-Raising & Malicious Mischief, Falsehood & Fraud) are generally headed 'Of Offences Against Property', as one might expect. But of greater present interest is the heading to chapters XVI and XVII, viz: 'Of Offences Against the Public Peace'. Of this group, the learned author simply states (at p 416): 'Another class of offences, little less interesting than those which we last examined [Offences Against the Course of Justice], consists of such as tend to the disturbance of the public peace'. It is highly significant that he purports to be dealing here with a '*class*' of offences, and indeed offences that '*tend*' to disturb the peace.

1.04   The particular heading 'Of Offences Against the Public Peace' was taken by Hume (see vol I at p 19) from *Blackstone's Commentaries on the Laws of England*, and it is instructive perhaps to consider what that eminent eighteenth century English judge wrote of the subjects of his inquiry thereunder. The important passage is this (at Bk IV, Ch 11, p 142): 'We are next to consider offences against the public *peace*, the conservation of which is intrusted to the king and his officers in the manner and for the reasons which were formerly mentioned at large. These offences are either such as are an actual breach of the peace; or constructively so, by tending to make others break it. Both of these species are also either felonious, or not felonious.' As Hume was always quick to point out where the laws of Scotland and England differed, it seems reasonable to assume that his silence in relation to the passage just quoted indicates no dissent from its adequacy as a description of his own understanding of this particular class of offences. Thus, *Breach of the Peace* is here presented as a general description of a class of offences — offences, some of them serious, which are connected in that the conduct involved effects a disturbance of the peace or tends to do so (*Hume*) or tends to make others do so (*Blackstone*). This may be thought of as the *wide* view of breach of the peace, since it seems possible that there is also a narrow view.

1.05 Hume's Chapter XVII (under the same general heading) begins with the following, much-quoted passage (at p 439):

'In familiar discourse, and sometimes, but rather improperly, in the proceedings of the inferior courts, which have the ordinary cognisance of such disturbances, the name of riot is also given to a mere brawl, or occasional quarrel and strife, among persons who were not assembled with any mischievous purpose. If, however, a contest of this sort happens in such a place, or is carried to such a length, as to disturb and alarm the neighbourhood, this seems to be cognisable at instance of the public prosecutor, as a breach of the public peace; to the effect at least of inflicting a fine and imprisonment, and exacting caution from the offenders, for their good behaviour for the future.'

This minor form of mobbing and rioting (see **1.08** ff, below) is possibly describable as a narrow form of breach of the peace, since it actually refers to that appellation *as if a nomen juris*. But it will be noted that Hume describes such a brawl as 'a' breach of the public peace, and not in terms that it is the only legitimate form capable of being brought under such a title. It probably goes too far, therefore, to state that 'Hume deals with breach of the peace in two sentences', as *Gordon* does (at p 985, fn 1) when quoting the passage reproduced immediately above. It must also be noted that this 'narrow' form of the crime is not confined explicitly to conduct in public places. Also, though Hume's writings must not be looked upon as if statutory in form, it is a moot point whether the words 'as to' convey the sense of causing in actuality disturbance and alarm, or whether they connote the mere likelihood of such a result. If the former is the true meaning, then this must indeed be a special, narrow form of breach of the peace offences, since the description (at p 416) of the whole class, it will be recalled, refers to offences which 'tend to the disturbance of the public peace'.

1.06 The conspectus of wide and narrow forms of these offences has some support from early nineteenth century works on the jurisdiction and powers of justices of the peace. In Blair's *Scottish Justices' Manual* (1834), for example, it is stated (at p 32) that '[i]n a general sense, every violation of public tranquility and order may be termed a breach of the peace ... But in a more limited meaning, it is applied to "a mere brawl, or occasional quarrel and strife among persons who were not assembled with any mischievous purpose"' (quoting directly from *Hume*). On the other hand, Hutcheson's *Treatise on the Office of*

Justice of Peace (1809), while agreeing that there is a narrow and extensive sense of breaches of the peace, gives a characteristically eccentric account of each in exceptionally wide and rather unhelpful terms (see pp 344–5). He does conclude, however, (at p 345) that breaches of the peace are multifarious, differ in their features, character, and consequences, and 'do not correctly admit any one definition'. This seems a not inaccurate account of how things stood in the early nineteenth century, and suggests that the wide view was essentially the correct one. (The narrow view was strongly contended for by the appellants in *Deakin v Milne* (1882) 5 Coup 174; but the High Court rejected any such restricted view.)

The wide nineteenth century view

1.07 Hume's class of offences against the public peace (see vol I, p 416) comprises those crimes which tend to disturb that peace. Within that class, he particularly mentions mobbing (ch XVI), the Sending of Threatening Letters, the Making of Verbal Threats, Challenging Persons to a Duel, the Bearing of Unlawful Weapons, and Brawling (as set out above at **1.05**). The latter five of these occupy chapter XVII. There is, however, no reason to believe that the instances expressly mentioned were meant by Hume to form a closed class, especially since items included under other of his general headings may also 'tend to disturb the public peace' (see **1.17** ff, below). But the specific examples will be considered first.

Mobbing and rioting

1.08 This was, and probably still is, the 'most eminent' (*Hume*, vol I, p 416) of the offences against the public peace, and proves that breaches of the peace are not all minor crimes. Hume's exposition of this crime (ch XVI), not disputed or matched in its comprehensiveness by any other contemporary writer, runs to three basic requirements. Mobbing ('rioting' being used as a synonym, see for example p 419) required first a large crowd of persons. There was no exact minimum number; but the smaller the number, the more outrageous in actuality the conduct of the crowd would have to be in order to qualify as 'mobbing'. (Conversely, the larger the number, the less would be the requirement of actual violence or outrage, since in the case of 'a great host or multitude . . . the very assembly is itself a terror and subject of alarm' — *Hume* vol I, p 416.) Secondly (and also at p 416), the crowd had to inspire fear in the lieges and disturb the public peace. But that disturbance had to be of a sufficiently serious degree. Hume's illustrations (p 419) as to when that degree might be reached (or perhaps deemed to be reached) are concerned with acts of destruction of, or damage to property; violent enterings ('invadings') of premises; personal injuries; pursuits of individuals with the intent 'to abuse, confine or put them in fear'; violent constraint or intimidations of particular persons; making plain a purpose to engage in 'some violent enterprise', provided some steps were actually taken towards implement thereof; and, even more broadly (at p 420), the mere assembling of a crowd for a violent purpose, where that purpose was (presumably) plain *and* where there was also (perhaps by sheer weight of numbers or by dint of disorderly commotion) disturbance of the peace of the neighbourhood and actual alarm caused to individuals. (It is noteworthy from these instances that most of them from their very nature would be taken as productive of the necessary degree of disturbance without actual proof thereof.) It followed from the foregoing that, thirdly, the persons assembled must have had a 'purpose of violence or mischief' (p 419), which entailed hostility to the peace of the neighbourhood (p 418) and which might be an end in itself, or a means to some other end. The purpose need not have been formed *ab ante*; it was enough if it arose plainly at some time during the assemblage of the crowd. *Alison* (vol I, p 513) refers to this requirement as that of a 'common purpose' or 'common design', a mode of reference which has become the norm. Purpose or design here must be taken, one imagines, as an intent, and it was (and is) the presence of such an intention (to do violence or to intimidate by force or sheer pressure of numbers, for example) which formed (and forms) the essence of the crime. Indeed, it was decided at an early point in the nineteenth century that the common purpose (object or design) must be plainly stated on the face of the (pre 1887) indictment (see *Francis Docherty* (1841) 2 Swin 635). But that purpose need never have been translated into action, provided there was about it a plain tendency to violence or mischief which reasonably caused alarm as to what *might* be done. The purpose then was all important.

1.09 Without such a purpose, there might still be a breach of the peace — but it would then be one 'of a lower kind' (*Hume*, vol I, p 418), which Hume referred to generally as a casual affray, a sudden brawl (or quarrel), or an occasional outrage (p 418; see also *Alison*, vol I, p 513) and which he dealt with more fully in another chapter (ch XVII at p 439; see **1.05**, above). These 'purposeless' offences he refers to, in the loose language of the lower courts of his day, as 'riots' (as does *Erskine*, Institute, Bk I, tit IV, para 4). Alison's view that 'rioting' was the name given to the outrageous conduct of an individual (vol I, p 510) seems highly dubious. Hume's view — that 'rioting' was yet another term for mobbing, and that a 'riot' was a convenient one-word expression for a more minor form of disturbance than mobbing — is supported by other writers (eg *Blair* (1834) at p 173) and by early case reports (eg *Wightman v Montgomery* (1758) Maclaurin 188, see **1.15**, below).

1.10   In essence, therefore, it is tempting to conclude that the difference between mobbing and many other forms of breach of the peace was one of dole in the early nineteenth century; that rioting required essentially the demonstration of an intent to disturb the peace of a particular locality (by virtue of the existence of a common purpose entailing, for whatever end, violence or intimidation), whereas other breaches of the peace did not. This would strongly suggest that most forms of breach of the peace required no dole — in the sense that accused persons need not be shown to have set out, or continued upon their conduct with any intent of disturbing the neighbourhood. It was enough that their conduct did effect such a disturbance or had a plain tendency to do so. Hume does not say this, however; and in any event, had all breaches of the peace required dole, there would have been little difficulty (as now) in finding it. Dole was (and still tends to be) 'determined by the nature of the act and its evil consequences to the public' (*Hume*, vol I, p 25) — ie it was (and is) determined by reference to objective criteria.

Threats as breaches of the peace

1.11   In Hume's view (vol I, pp 439–442), certain types of threat were prosecutable as offences against the public peace. Written threats conveyed by letter were certainly within that class if the threats concerned fire-raising or other 'great mischief' (p 439). The impression is also given that where such a letter was an anonymous one, the required seriousness of the threat might be somewhat less; but all the examples listed couple threats with demands for money or other advantages. How extortionate demands of such a nature amount, or tend, to disturbances of the public peace is far from clear. Such conduct seems aimed solely at the individual rather than a wider audience — unless, of course, every crime is to be considered as a breach of the peace. But Hume does not suggest that; and indeed such a view is neither tenable nor in accordance with practical reality.

Further, many specific offences lack the immediate potential for public disturbance — and are thus distanced from, for example, mobbing or sudden affrays. In the case of *John Jaffray* (1815, Hume, vol I, p 441, fn 2), however, the recipient of an incendiary letter was not himself the subject of the threats, which were directed at a number of other people. It could certainly be argued there that there was an element of public alarm, or at least the likelihood of it. Also in that case, there were already circumstances of public alarm, since there had been other, contemporary instances of fire-raising in the area (Kelso). The accused, therefore, could have been said to be fuelling a given situation of public alarm or disturbance. But the situation was clearly a special one.

1.12 With verbal threats, the situation is perhaps a clearer one. As Hume states (at p 442):

'[E]ven the verbal threatening of personal mischief, if violent and pointed, is a relevant ground of alarm, both to the individual and the public, for obliging the offender to find caution to keep the complainer free of harm'.

Certainly, an uttered threat of personal violence (assuming that to be meant by the phrase 'personal mischief') carries with it an immediate potential for alarm and disturbance. Blows may be landed. There may be retaliation. There may be escalation of the violence by dint of assistance materialising for either side. But there must, of course, be a violent threat. Offensive words *per se* would not partake of that requirement, as Hume makes clear elsewhere (see vol I, ch X — Of Offences Against Reputation — at pp 340–344). Thus, to call a person a thief or a whore or an adulterer would truly be a civil and not a criminal matter, if such utterances were 'loose and passionate appellations' (p 341). The matter might be different if, for example, a person were to be labelled as a thief in respect of a specific instance of theft. But apart from such instances of saddling a person with the guilt of a specific offence out of sheer malice rather than conviction (*animo injuriandi*), loose and passionate verbal 'assaults' *per se* were not criminal in Hume's estimation — either as breaches of the peace or anything else. Where slanderous expressions were mixed with violent threats, the matter might, of course, be different. As Hume remarked (p 343):

'The only other situation I know of, where criminal process has been sustained, at instance of an individual, for injurious words thrown out against him, is where the words are uttered in his presence, and are attended with such circumstances of rage and disturbance, as justly to alarm with the fear of further mischief; so that it is not a case of pure slander, but savours of violence, and has a tendency towards a real assault.'

Such a case occurred in *Hamilton, Lady St Foord v Gordon* (1708, 1709) Hume, vol I, pp 343–4, and fn 2, where a charge against Gordon of having called the complainer a common whore, an adulterous bitch, and the bearer of an illegitimate child, as also having threatened her with blows if she should answer back, was held *separatim* relevant to infer an arbitrary punishment (although he had further at the time been engaged in violently dispossessing her of certain poinded goods). It may well be opined that an innominate type of breach of the peace was what the Lords of Justiciary here had in mind, since this would be consistent with Hume's approach to verbal threats.

Challenges to duels

1.13   These, according to Hume (at p 442), 'may properly be considered as a breach of the peace'. He here was thinking, however, of challenges to mortal combat, as forbidden under certain statutes of the Scots Parliament (ie 1600 c 12 [APS IV c 21, p 230]; 1696 c 35 [APS X c 37, p 77]) which appointed Draconian penalties therefor. This all seems rather far removed from public disturbance or alarm, real or likely. It also seems far removed from challenges to an instant fight without weapons. But Alison (vol I, p 580) points out that the old statutes in question were repealed by 59 Geo III c 70 (now itself repealed by the Statute Law Revision Act 1873, c 91), and that the matter thenceforth rested on the common law which was 'amply sufficient to reach and punish all such breaches or attempted breaches of the peace'. (Given the width of Hume's conception of breach of the peace, it is hard to see what Alison can mean by an *attempted* breach, unless it be a challenge to fight *simpliciter* which is not followed by actual fighting. But if offences of this class need only tend to public disturbance (*Hume*, vol I, p 416), what clearer instance of an actual breach of the peace could there be?)

Bearing of unlawful weapons

1.14   Similarly, the open carrying by non-armed-services personnel (or in modern times by persons other than the police) of weapons capable of killing must surely be the occasion of public alarm and disturbance. But Hume discusses this aspect of breach of the peace not with respect to the common law, but with reference to certain Scots statutes of the seventeenth century (vol I, pp 444–5). As he admits that these statutes were probably in desuetude even in *Mackenzie's* time, it is difficult to draw firm conclusions from this aspect of his exposition.

A short description of Hume's breach of the peace

1.15 It seems clear, then, that Hume did not treat breach of the peace as a single, unitary offence. Rather he saw it as the general title to be adhibited to a group of innominate offences which had in common the feature of public disturbance and alarm. With the exception of mobbing, the use of a *nomen juris* was optional, since a description of what had been done and an assertion of actual disturbance, or the likelihood of same in consequence, seemed to have been enough — especially so since breaches of the peace were most often dealt with before the inferior courts (see **1.16**, below), where technical precision was not held at a premium. Again with the probable exception of mobbing, dole appears to have been largely irrelevant, and the offences themselves often fairly trivial. Finally, there appeared to be no requirement that the conduct in question should itself have occurred in a public place. In *Wightman v Montgomery* (1758) Maclaurin 188, for example, no exception was taken, although the facts were disputed, to the following being described as a 'riot' in a private house:

'[T]hat there had been for a considerable time, a great tumult and disturbance in a house in the neighbourhood, by people fighting, cursing, swearing, singing idle songs, vomiting over the window, and calling out the most obscene language to women who were passing, which was the occasion of the people assembling, and did give great offence to all who heard it.'

Of course, there was a wider public effect of the conduct complained of, which is not without significance. Also significant is the labelling of cursing, swearing and other *offensive* conduct (both actual and verbal) as 'acts of riot'; for these seem *ex facie* to be foreign to Hume's description of breaches of the peace. There are probably two connected reasons for this, however. First, most breaches of the peace were dealt with in the inferior courts (see **1.16**, below), and, secondly, potential for disturbance and alarm was a feature of certain offences dealt with by Hume under headings other than breach of the peace (see **1.17**, below).

Breach of the peace and the inferior courts

1.16 With the exception of mobbing, the class of offences against the public peace was generally one for the attention of the inferior courts. In *Hume* (vol II, p 147), the inferior judicatories are described as the Sheriff, Burgh and Justice of Peace courts (see also *Erskine*, Institute, vol I, bk I, tit IV, paras 4, 13; *Alison*, vol II, Introduction, p xiii), and (at p 60 ff) the respective jurisdictions of these courts are described to varying degrees of precision. It is clear, however, that they all might deal with affrays, brawls and outrages in the street, and that it was the duty of the judges of these courts (and their officers) to maintain the peace within their bounds. It will be recalled also, that in volume I (ch XVII at p 439) Hume had remarked that the inferior courts had 'the ordinary cognisance of such disturbances' as were commonly but loosely called riots. Add to that Alison's statement (vol II, Introduction, p xiii) that petty offences against the public peace were dealt with summarily by these courts, and it follows that precision in libelling such offences was hardly to be looked for — so long as disturbances and alarm were evident or likely as a result of what was said to have been done in any particular case. There was little incentive, therefore, to define such crimes precisely (let alone narrowly), and perhaps every reason to maximise the powers of those inferior courts in their task of maintaining the peace. Mobbing, on the other hand, being a serious example of breach of the peace and often before the Lords of Justiciary, was much more clearly defined, since indictments or criminal letters were involved and the premisses set out thereunder had to pass the stringent tests of relevancy.

Offences against the public police

1.17 In his classification of crimes, Hume places those dealt with in chapters XVIII to XXII under the heading 'Offences Against the Public Police and Economy'. Once again (see **1.04**, above) this heading is taken from *Blackstone* whose explanation is reproduced and adopted (at p 446). It is worth quoting the passage in full (*Blackstone's Commentaries*, bk IV, ch 13, p 162 at V):

'The last species of offences which especially affect the commonwealth are those against the *public police* and *oeconomy*. By the public police and oeconomy I mean that due regulation and domestic order of the kingdom: whereby the individuals of the state, like members of a well-governed family, are bound to conform their general behaviour to the rules of propriety, good neighbourhood, and good manners; and to be decent, industrious, and inoffensive in their respective stations. This head of offences must therefore be very miscellaneous, as it comprises all such crimes as especially affect public society... These amount, some of them to felony, and others to misdemeanours only.'

1.18 In the above quotation, we have the concept of the 'police offence', much referred to in nineteenth century cases, where it is often distinguished from the concept of breach of the peace (eg see *Banks v M'Lennan* (1876) 3 Coup 359 at 361–2, per Lord Young; *Hendry v Ferguson* (1883) 5 Coup 278 at 282, per Lord Justice-Clerk Moncrieff). Since offences of this description are very various, it is not easy to see wherein the connection lies. Hume, for example, lists Incest (ch xviii); Adultery (ch XIX); Bigamy and Clandestine Marriage (ch XX); Fornication, Excessive Drinking, Unnatural Lusts (only sodomy and bestiality being considered thereunder, cf *R v HM Advocate* 1988 SCCR 254) and Brothel Keeping (ch XXI); and, being a Blackmailer or a Vagabond of various sorts (ch XXII) — some of these being statutorily based offences. But, consideration of contemporary meanings of the word 'police' sheds some light on the matter. The Oxford English Dictionary (1933 edn) lists two obsolete significances which were both in use in the late eighteenth and early nineteenth centuries, and were indeed used in those senses by Erskine (s.v. 'Police', I.1, II.2 and illustrations from *Erskine*). In the first of these, 'police' means simply 'policy'. Thus offences against the public police could comprise the wide class of offences contrary to public policy. Hume's examples (quoted above) and Blackstone's own words (also quoted above, at **1.17**) certainly lend themselves to that sort of interpretation. (But equally, it could be said rather unhelpfully that all offences — common law ones at least — are ones contrary to public policy.) The second contemporary meaning refers to the discipline and control of a community and lends itself more narrowly to the concept of public order. It is more likely than not that this is what Hume, Blackstone, Erskine and certain nineteenth century judges mainly had in mind. They mainly had in mind situations of minor public disorder, or conduct which, in Blackstone's words, amounted to 'common nuisance' (*Commentaries*, bk IV, ch 13, p 167). The underlying feeling here might well have been that conduct which caused public annoyance or offence, or constituted a gross departure from ordinary moral norms ought to be reachable by the criminal law. But such conduct need not, of course, amount to some minor matter for the inferior courts (cf incest, for example, or the sort of conduct recently condemned by the Appeal Court in *R v H M Advocate* 1988 SCCR 254); and other likely candidates for Hume's class of 'Public Police' have oddly been inserted elsewhere in his scheme. Cursing and swearing, for example, appears under the heading 'Offences Against Religion' (ch XXIX) as also, rather more understandably, does blasphemy.

1.19   Nevertheless, it appears from the available evidence that an offence against the public police was primarily seen as a minor one involving disorderly conduct, or annoyance (as opposed to alarm), or a departure from generally accepted standards of decency or propriety. Such offences could be described as 'violations of the duty of a decent and well disposed citizen' (*Hume*, I, ch XVIII, p 446).

1.20   A problem lay, however, in the close connection between some of these police offences and offences which were breaches of the public peace. Cursing and swearing, for example, might cause mere annoyance or offence; but, depending on the circumstances and on what was said, it might more seriously be productive of alarm and disturbance. It might, therefore, properly be placed in either camp according to circumstances. (Hume treats cursing and swearing as 'offences against religion' since there were statutes of the Scots Parliament (now repealed) which penalised *profane* swearing, a specialised form of the 'art'.) Throughout the nineteenth century, this close connection was reflected in a tendency to ignore the separate class of offences against the public police, and to treat examples from that class as if they belonged to the category of breaches of the peace. As that tendency became commonplace, the already wide class of breach of the peace was enlarged still further, with resultant confusion between offences designed to maintain order and propriety and those concerned with public disturbance and alarm.

Powers of arrest for breach of the peace

1.21   Hume (vol II, pp 75–7) lays it down as a matter of common law that any judge of the inferior courts (see **1.16**, above), who had personal knowledge of the same, might summarily arrest a person suspected of having committed a felony, 'or even' (p 75) a riot or breach of the peace. Similarly, a constable might do so, and he might even force entry to premises where a suspected felon had taken refuge from pursuit — but not where the suspect was believed only to have committed a breach of the peace. Private persons might also exercise powers of summary arrest, but only where the suspicion concerned 'an attrocious felony'. A private person had no power to arrest on suspicion of a 'mere' (p 77) breach of the peace. These powers are probably still competent at common law; but Hume's treatment of them serves to emphasise that the majority of breaches of the peace were to be reckoned as minor crimes.

Drunkenness as mitigation

1.22 Hume's views on drunkenness as an issue in criminal law are well known. Far from being an excuse, it might be regarded as an aggravation of any crime committed under its influence (vol I, p 45); but in practice, it would simply be ignored in the case of an intoxicated accused and not 'save him from the ordinary pains of his transgression'. Indeed, drunkenness 'itself shews a disregard of order and decency' (p 46), and thus is really *per se* a police offence (see **1.17** ff, above; *Blair* (1834), p 79).

1.23 Nevertheless, in certain cases of crime 'which are neither attended with any profit to the delinquent, nor any *necessary* or immediate damage to one's neighbour, or to society; and which are chiefly reputed criminal, on account of the violation of order and decency, and the *possible* evil influence on the minds of others' (p 46), it is envisaged by Hume that intoxication (presumably self-induced) may be used in mitigation of sentence. The examples he specifically refers to are somewhat arcane — blasphemy, heresy, leasing-making and the uttering of seditious words. But, at p 47, he does venture the opinion that: 'Many other instances may be imagined, which seem to offer the like reasons for mitigation of the ordinary pains . . .'. It is possible, therefore, that this provides some authority for pleading intoxication by way of mitigation in answer to a charge of shouting and swearing, or minor disorderly conduct, or minor lewdness — as indeed is often done today.

Conclusion

1.24 Breach of the peace, therefore, was not a particular offence with a well-defined meaning in the early nineteenth century. It was more properly the name of a *genus* of innominate offences which caused, or could reasonably be expected to cause, public disturbance and alarm. Most such offences were minor and addressed to the inferior courts, where precision in the drawing of charges was not required. Also, in those courts, police offences were dealt with — ie those offences which were concerned with annoyance, offensiveness and the maintenance of standards of propriety and decency. There was a natural tendency for these to be dealt with as if part of the class of breach of the peace, which gave rise to the impression that that class was even more extensive than perhaps it should have been.

1.25   One would not wish to advance this situation as necessarily a happy one, nor to exhibit the same as a laudable facet of the operation of common law. But it should be appreciated that some of the most criticised features of breach of the peace were already built into the crime (or species of crimes) before the nineteenth and twentieth century case-law even began.

II General issues

Statutory forms and rules: relevancy

2.01 On the assumption that the vast majority of breaches of the peace will be prosecuted summarily (see **2.08**, below), it is probably enough to consider the rules in Part II of the Criminal Procedure (Scotland) Act 1975. Thus in terms of s 312, the

'[c]harge in a complaint under this Part of this Act *shall* be stated in the form, as nearly as may be, of the appropriate form contained in Part II of Schedule 2 to the Summary Jurisdiction (Scotland) Act 1954 or in an Act of Adjournal under this Act. No further specification shall be required than a specification similar to that given in that form and . . . (b) it shall not be necessary to specify by any *nomen juris* the offence which is charged, but it shall be sufficient that the complaint sets forth facts relevant and sufficient to constitute an offence punishable on complaint.'

2.02 Statutory forms of criminal charges have been laid down since 1887 (for indictments and complaints) and since 1908 (specifically for complaints). Apart from mobbing, Schedule A of the 1887 Criminal Procedure (Scotland) Act contains no styles appropriate to breach of the peace. The appropriate styles are presently to be found in the 1954 Act, no Act of Adjournal for such purposes having yet been enacted. There are three such styles, viz: —

'You did conduct yourself in a disorderly manner and commit a breach of the peace; You did threaten violence to the lieges and commit a breach of the peace; [and,] You did fight and commit a breach of the peace'.

2.03 Provided that the substance of one or other of these styles is employed, and provided that a *locus* and a date are declared for the alleged offence, a complaint for breach of the peace cannot be irrelevant on the ground of want of specification (*HM Advocate v James Swan* (1888) 2 White 137 at 144, per Lord Justice-Clerk Macdonald; his words relate specifically to styles under the 1887 Act, but are also of general application). In the particular instance of 'conducting oneself in a disorderly manner', this entails approval of a charge which *ex facie* provides no advance information as to the precise case the

15

accused has to meet. However unfair that may appear, it nevertheless follows from one possible interpretation of section 312 — an interpretation which has now received both the tacit (eg *Craig v Herron* (1976) SCCR Supp 152; *Wilson v Brown* 1982 SLT 361 (Note); *Alexander v Smith* 1984 SLT 176 (Note)) and express approval of the Appeal Court (*Anderson v Allan* 1985 SCCR 399; *Butcher v Jessop* 1989 SCCR 119; and see also *Gardiner v Jones* (1890) 2 White 474, approving the 'conduct yourself in a disorderly manner' style found relevant in *Bewglass v Blair* (1888) 1 White 574). To circumvent criticism that such approval is in breach of the 'fair notice' principle, the court has opined that the accused may always precognosce all the witnesses on the prosecution's list (*Anderson v Allan* at pp 400–401). Alternatively, in particular instances, it may be quite obvious what the substance of the Crown's case amounts to (as was claimed and upheld in *Butcher v Jessop*); but where there is doubt, and perhaps in any event as a matter of sound practice, defence agents would appear to have a duty to precognosce in 'disorderly conduct' cases, *quantum valeat*. It remains just possible, perhaps, in extreme instances, to argue that the bare statutory style provides insufficient notice of the case to be answered by the defence. As much is said by Lord Murray in *Butcher v Jessop* (at 134A). It should be remembered, however, that his opinion is in essence a dissenting one and that his example (of a man being charged by the police in respect of a disturbance outside a public house and subsequently finding at trial that his 'disorderly conduct' charge includes 'peeping tom' activities) is somewhat extreme. Certainly it has been held that 'conducting oneself in a disorderly manner' will include acts of violence, and that evidence in support of such acts must be anticipated in an appropriate case (*Butcher v Jessop*, eg Lord Justice-Clerk Ross at 129B).

2.04   The conclusion here is that charges which follow the statutory styles are unlikely to be considered irrelevant. For this reason, it is now almost universal practice to favour the 'conduct yourself in a disorderly manner' form. This may or may not be supplemented with additional information — as the prosecutor sees fit (see, for example, the complaint in *Thompson v MacPhail* 1989 SCCR 266, which Lord Brand (at 268D) considered to leave 'so much to conjecture'). Any supplemental allegations are, however, just that. They do not restrict the wide scope of 'conducting oneself in a disorderly manner' (*Boyle v Wilson* 1988 SCCR 485). But whatever style is adopted, the Crown must still prove its case. A submission of 'no case to answer' under s 345A of the Criminal Procedure (Scotland) Act 1975 is, therefore, likely to be attended with greater success than any objection to relevancy, unless there is major departure from the statutory forms.

Even where there is such departure (eg in *Winnik v Allan* 1986 SCCR
35, where the very words of style 'conduct yourself in a disorderly
manner' were deleted by the sheriff, without apparent damage to the
relevancy of the charge), there are so many forms of charge which
have met with approval over the last century and a half that the success
of an objection to relevancy remains questionable. (So unusual are
pleas to the relevancy *quoad* this offence that in *MacNeill v Robertson*
1982 SCCR 468, where the form of the charge was unusual and
suspect, it was the sheriff himself who raised the matter of its irrelevancy.)

Breach of the peace as a *nomen juris*

2.05   Despite the terms of s 312(b) of the Criminal Procedure (Scotland) Act 1975 (see **2.01**, above), all the statutory styles (and indeed
almost all modern charges) conclude with the words 'and did commit
a breach of the peace'. This gives the impression that a complaint
which failed to employ such words might be bad for uncertainty, in
that the appropriate *nomen juris* had not been used and therefore it was
unclear what precisely had been charged. Whether or not that would
amount to a worthwhile plea depends largely on what is stated in the
charge and the attitude of the sheriff, justice or stipendiary magistrate
involved. For example, in *Skeen v Peacock* (1970 SLT (Sh Ct) 66) the
accused was charged in terms that he did wilfully and maliciously
drive a car in front of a bus, cause the driver of the bus to brake sharply
to avoid a collision with that car, and did endanger the safety of the
bus driver and the occupants of the bus. The sheriff there upheld a
plea to the relevancy of the complaint on the basis that what was
charged was not a known crime in Scots law. In one sense, that
decision seems questionable, since the accused's conduct could certainly have been described as 'disorderly'; and there might clearly
have been alarm or annoyance experienced by the bus driver and his
passengers. Did the charge simply lack the words without which it
could not be relevant — viz: 'And did commit a breach of the peace'?
Of course, it must be borne in mind that prosecutors have wide
powers of amendment (under s 335(1) of the 1975 Act) of a defective
complaint. But such amendments will not be permitted if they change
the character of the offence charged (s 335(2)), and presumably any
attempt to alter a non-criminal charge to a valid one would constitute
such a change. Again, the relevancy of the charge in *Skeen v Peacock*
was never tested on appeal. If it had been, a relevant charge of breach
of the peace might conceivably have been found. Support for this view

can be found in *Dyce v Aitchison* (1985 SCCR 184), albeit the charge there was *ex facie* a clearer one. The charge in that case read:

'[o]n . . . at Inverness Sheriff Court . . . having been brought before the sheriff . . . to answer to a complaint [theft by housebreaking] you did conduct yourself in said . . . court in an improper and disorderly manner and did strike your fist hard on the dock where you were standing, swear and use obscene language, threaten violence towards Sheriff Booker-Milburn who was then on the bench . . . and did struggle violently with and resist police officers . . . who were removing you from the dock of said . . . court and in consequence of which improper and disorderly behaviour you are guilty of contempt of court.'

The prosecutor very properly (and successfully) sought leave to delete the words from 'and in consequence' to 'contempt of court', contempt not being a crime. Once that deletion had been made, it was strongly contended that what was left was bad for uncertainty. But the sheriff's rejection of that plea was upheld by the Appeal Court. Lord Justice-Clerk Wheatley said (at 188) that 'the complaint libels *species facti* which contain not one but two offences known to the law of Scotland', and he affirmed that no *nomen juris* need be mentioned in fact (under reference to s 312(b) of the 1975 Act). Unfortunately, neither he nor Lord Grieve (Lord Dunpark simply concurring) specified which two offences were contained within the amended complaint; but it must have been the case that breach of the peace was one of them.

2.06 So it would appear that 'breach of the peace' is now a *nomen juris* and *ex lege* need not be mentioned expressly in a complaint. Nor do the statutory styles create a *de facto* requirement for the inclusion of the words 'breach of the peace' in order that there might be a relevant charge.

The width of the crime

2.07 Despite the fact that breach of the peace is now regarded as a *nomen juris* rather than as a description of a class of offences (see **1.03**, above), the scope of the modern offence is as wide and possibly much wider than the contents of Hume's former class (see **1.07**, above). The 'narrow view' that the crime might properly be confined to quarrelling or strife has regularly been dismissed by the courts (eg *Deakin v Milne* (1882) 5 Coup 174; *Ferguson v Carnochan* (1889) 2 White 278). Also, no separate class of 'police offences' is now recognised at common law (see *Raffaelli v Heatly* 1949 SLT 284 at 285–6, per Lord Mackay) since 'police offences' have largely been subsumed by breach of the peace. A wide variety of conduct is, therefore, to be found under the 'breach of the peace' banner, to the extent that the Appeal Court has stated (in *Montgomery v McLeod* (1977) SCCR Supp 164 at 165):

'There is no limit to the kind of conduct which may give rise to a charge of breach of the peace. All that is required is that there must be some conduct such as to excite the reasonable apprehension to which we have drawn attention [viz. that mischief may ensue], or such as to create disturbance and alarm to the lieges in fact.'

In practice, of course, there is a limit. Since Scots law prides itself on being a 'common sense' system of criminal justice, this must be so. There will certainly be occasions when it would be absurd, unjust and contrary to good sense to categorise conduct as a breach of the peace, even where that conduct had indeed caused 'disturbance and alarm to the lieges in fact'. The victim of an attack, for example, may well by way of self-defence conduct himself in a way which disturbs and alarms the lieges — but it must surely be more than an exercise of prosecutorial discretion which renders him free from prosecution. Nevertheless, it must be conceded that this is an offence 'the limits of which have never been sharply defined. It is so largely in each case a question of circumstances and of degree' (*Young v Heatly* 1959 JC 66 at 70, per Lord Justice-General Clyde). As breach of the peace is a common law crime and part of a dynamic system of criminal law, that conclusion is either an advantage or the price that has to be paid. It is not a special characteristic of breach of the peace itself. As was observed many years ago by the first Lord Justice-General Clyde in *McLaughlan v Boyd* 1933 SLT 629 at 631:

'It would be a mistake to imagine that the criminal common law of Scotland countenances any precise and exact categorisation of the forms of conduct which amount to crime. It has been pointed out many times in this Court that such is not the nature or quality of the criminal law of Scotland.'

Is breach of the peace simply a minor crime?

2.08   All common law offences may be prosecuted summarily or on indictment at the discretion of the prosecutor. Such discretion will be exercised according to various criteria, one of which being the gravity of the alleged offence (Renton & Brown, *Criminal Procedure according to the Law of Scotland* (5th edn, 1983) para 3.02). As breach of the peace is a common law offence (see **1.01**, above), the matter of particular breaches being so serious as to merit solemn procedure arises for consideration. With the exception of mobbing and rioting (and making due allowance for acute recidivism), it is thought that breach of the peace is intrinsically a minor crime and should not *per se* be taken on indictment.

2.09   Certainly, in the nineteenth century, the view was taken that breach of the peace was not *per se* a fit matter for first-instance proceedings before the High Court. Thus Lord Deas (in *HM Advocate v Blair* (1868) 1 Coup 168 at 173) agreed that: '[I]t is quite true that breach of the peace, when it occurs by itself, is usually treated as a police offence and would not form alone a proper subject for indictment in this Supreme Court.' And Lord Justice-Clerk Moncreiff (in *McGuire v Fairbairn* (1881) 4 Coup 536 at 541) expressed the view, in an appeal against sentence for breach of the peace, that severe punishments (in this case five years in a reformatory school) were not 'intended to apply to the minor grades of crime, but only to those of graver complexion, such as theft or similar offences'. Again, in *Kelly v Rowan*, (1897) 2 Adam 357, where the accused had been kept in custody for seven days before being brought before a magistrate, Lord Justice-Clerk Macdonald remarked (at 361): 'The man was charged with a paltry offence — breach of the peace — and he was to be kept in prison for a time which would have been a severe punishment for such an offence, unless it was aggravated.'

2.10   Of course, breach of the peace may appear on an indictment along with more serious crimes (eg in *HM Advocate v Maitland* 1985 SLT 425, murder, theft, assault and other crimes were also charged; and in *Upton v HM Advocate* 1986 SCCR 188, the additional offence was that of attempting to defeat the ends of justice) and this is of regular and proper occurrence. On such an indictment, if a verdict of guilty of breach of the peace alone was to be returned, it is thought equally proper that the sentence should reflect the minor nature of that offence — irrespective of the powers of the sentencing court *quoad* common law crimes in general. There has, however, been one significant exception to this, as far as reported cases are concerned. It arises from the fact that breach of the peace is invariably involved in the wording of a mobbing and rioting charge. Since it is legitimate to convict of an offence which forms part of the narrative of another (Criminal Procedure (Scotland) Act 1975, s 61(2) — *quaere* whether breach of the peace is really an 'indictable crime'), and since mobbing requires certain essential features (such as 'purpose') which it may not always be possible to prove, it is not uncommon to convict of (or accept a plea of guilty to) breach of the peace on an indictment for mobbing. But the High Court has on occasion regarded such convictions as still serious (eg *John Duncan* (1843) 1 Broun 512) and not allowed particularly significant reductions from the tarriffs for mobbing (eg in *Peter & Ann Ross* (1854) 1 Irv 540, the male accused was sentenced to 18 months (after a plea of guilty to breach of the peace had been accepted on a mobbing indictment), as was the accused in *Thomas Whitfield* (1843) 1 Broun 609, whose plea of guilty to mobbing was accepted). Considering such convictions as serious and sentencing accordingly seems anomalous, especially since the difference between mobbing and breach of the peace is believed to be one of (significant) degree; and it is thought that in modern law, appropriate and real reductions in sentence should be made to reflect the minor crime which breach of the peace normally is. The opportunity should not be taken in such cases to regard the conviction as *de facto* one of mobbing, and to impose a sentence on that basis.

2.11 Because of the wide range of conduct which can be brought under a charge of breach of the peace, it is inevitable that some *ex facie* 'breaches' may also come within the domain of some other crime. The relationship between breach of the peace and mobbing provides the most obvious, but not the only example. Thus, fighting and brawling may involve assault. The writing and sending of threatening letters of sufficient seriousness has come to be regarded as a crime in its own right (cf **1.07**, above). Lewd conduct, especially towards children, which involves more active behaviour than indecent remarks, will be seen as the separate offence of lewd, indecent and libidinous practices. The criterion in these cases as to whether breach of the peace or some other crime ought to be charged relates to the gravity of the conduct in the circumstances. As Henry H Brown put the matter in 1895 ('Breach of the Peace', 3 SLT 151 at 153): '[T]he proper course seems to be that trivial cases should be charged as breaches of the peace, and more serious cases as substantive offences'. His point is perhaps well illustrated in *Darroch v HM Advocate* (1980 SLT 33) where the accused was charged on indictment with repeatedly making phone calls in which he threatened to throw petrol bombs through the windows of his victim's house and car. He was also alleged to have threatened the victim and his family with more conventional assaults, and to have thrown a piece of metal through a window of the victim's house, thus placing the occupants in a state of fear and alarm for their safety. Although this could have been charged as breach of the peace, the gravity alone of the conduct would have suggested more serious charges (eg criminal threats and malicious mischief); and the circumstances — viz. that the victim had been due to give evidence against the accused in a solemn trial, and that the intention was to dissuade him from giving that evidence — made it plain that the correct way to proceed was by narrating the events and charging the accused with attempting to pervert the course of justice.

2.12   The general conclusion then is that breach of the peace is not a suitable appellation unless the accused's offence can be regarded as a minor one. It is, therefore, primarily an offence for the summary courts. Great faith is, of course, reposed in Scottish prosecutors to exercise fairly and properly the wide discretion which they have. But if they fail to do so, and charge such a minor crime on indictment by itself, it is not clear what might be done. Public prosecutors proceeding by way of indictment are privileged in what they do (*Renton & Brown*, para 21-06). Pleas to either the competency or relevancy would appear to be inappropriate (*Renton & Brown*, para 9-18 ff). It might be possible to request a preliminary diet so that the question of oppression might be aired. As is stated in *Renton & Brown* (para 9-35): 'The court retains an inherent power to dismiss a prosecution where the Crown have acted oppressively, although the power is one which will be rarely exercised'. The decided cases on oppression, however, have been concerned with inordinate delays in process and not with the point raised here. A court may also, of course, desert a diet of trial *simpliciter*; but this would be a drastic (and unlikely) step for it to take, which the prosecutor could in any event appeal against. A petition to the *nobile officium* might also be considered. But in the final analysis, a reduction of a charge from indictment to complaint-status on the ground that breach of the peace is but a minor crime would seem almost impossible to achieve without the active concurrence of the Crown. There is also an increasing trend to use breach of the peace as a weapon against football hooliganism. To emphasise to the individuals concerned and to the wider public the potential (or actual) seriousness of such conduct, there has been recent deliberate use of solemn procedure for breaches of the peace. The thinking clearly is that condign punishments deter. Whether or not that is justified thinking, the use of breach of the peace as an indictable offence in such circumstances attracts considerable public and judicial sympathy. One must also, of course, sympathise with the Crown's position, in that unruly behaviour at large-crowd sporting events may not easily be pigeonholed as assault or mobbing or indeed any other traditionally serious crime. But resort to breach of the peace in such cases illustrates the extraordinary flexibility of that crime, as also the lack of anything more suitable either at common law or under statute to deal with the realities of the situation. (The same may also be said of the increasing use of breach of the peace on indictment in cases of prison disturbances — see, for example, *Ralston v HM Advocate* 1988 SCCR 590.)

Despite such trends, breach of the peace is still in popular and general legal conception a minor crime; but increasing (as opposed to exceptional) use of solemn procedure will inevitably entail reconsideration of its status.

Trivial conduct

2.13 If breach of the peace (with the exception of the special case of mobbing) is essentially a minor offence, the question arises whether there is conduct which a court might regard as too trivial to warrant proceedings. Certain nineteenth century case decisions carry *obiter* remarks which suggest that that might be so. In *Stevenson v Lang* ((1878) 4 Coup 76) for example, Lord Craighill (at pp 82–3) was emphatically dismissive of a charge of which the substance involved the throwing of pease meal and soot in a Glasgow street — had it been charged at common law. As he said:

'The appellant's conduct is said to have been riotous and disorderly, but all that was done was to throw a certain quantity of pease meal and soot into the air. No doubt this is followed up by the statement that there was thus created annoyance and disturbance; how or why this result ensued is not explained. But assuming that there was such a consequence, and that it might be brought under the cognisance of the magistrate sitting in the police court as an offence under the provisions of the Glasgow Police Act 1866 [s 135(5)], I am still of opinion that it is not a good cause of complaint against anyone if the complaint is founded, not upon that statute [as in fact it was], but upon the rules of the common law.'

It seems, therefore, that Lord Craighill would have found that complaint too trivial for breach of the peace. But, speaking as he was in the years before the existence of standard, statutory forms of summary charges, he may simply have been concerned with the lack of specification in the particular complaint before him. In any event, the remarks are clearly *obiter*; and the way in which local (and general) burgh statutes could once have been relied upon to bolster up common law crimes no longer applies — the suspicion being that the trivial offences contained within those now repealed statutes have now passed to the province of breach of the peace (along with the more minor common law 'police offences').

2.14 Where the conduct is trivial, there are of course alternatives to prosecution — such as fiscals' warning letters (see 1979 SLT (News) 279). But there is every reason to believe that trivial behaviour is often prosecuted as breach of the peace. For example, in *Craig v Herron*

((1976) SCCR Supp 152), a motorist had blown his horn at a taxi-cab which suddenly pulled over into the lane occupied by that motorist's car. There may or may not have been a good reason for the taxi-cab's doing so. Its driver, however, was incensed and stopped his vehicle in such a way as to bring the motorist's vehicle to a halt. He then called the motorist an idiot and lectured him on the standard of his driving. There was nothing more to it than that. The High Court, however, upheld the taxi driver's conviction for breach of the peace, although they remarked (p 153) that 'this particular offence of breach of the peace was of a somewhat technical character and of trivial significance looking at the run of cases of this type...'. For good measure, the original fine of £15 was reduced to £5 '[t]o mark the true relationship between this offence and offences of breach of the peace generally...'. In short, it was trivial; but it was not in any way questionable to deal with it by prosecution and conviction.

General definitions of breach of the peace

2.15 Although the Appeal Court has generally been wary of assigning precise definitions to common law crimes, there have been attempts to define breach of the peace in a general way. Apart from Hume's account of the class of breaches of the peace (an account — see **1.15**, above — which the courts have largely ignored), a handful of case decisions has been regarded with particular favour from the point of view of definition. The earliest of these cases is *Ferguson v Carnochan* ((1889) 2 White 278, 16 R (J) 93, 26 SLR 624). It is not really surprising that this case should have been so thoroughly mined for statements of authority. The opinions of the Lord Justice-Clerk (Macdonald) and Lord McLaren appear in such different forms in the two leading versions of the report (ie in 2 White and 16 R (J) — 26 SLR generally following Rettie) as to enable a wide variety of interpretations to be formed. It is most perplexing that accounts purportedly of the same opinions should be at such variance (see the opinions set out in parallel in the Appendix). Nor has there ever been any agreement as to which version should be preferred (assuming, of course, that the differences have been noted and appreciated). Of the more recent decisions on breach of the peace which have sought to rely on *Ferguson v Carnochan*, some (eg *Raffaelli v Heatly* 1949 SLT 284 at 286, per Lord Mackay; *Wilson v Brown* 1982 SCCR 49 at 51, per Lord Dunpark) have relied on the Justiciary Cases version, and some (eg *Young v Heatly* 1959 JC 66 at 70, per Lord Justice-General Clyde; *Taylor v Hamilton* 1984 SCCR 393 at 395, per Sheriff Forbes's Note) on that which appears in 2 White. Neither version in fact seems without blemish, and the reader must judge for himself which is the better (or how the two may be fitted together to make some sense).

2.16   The facts of *Ferguson v Carnochan* are well known. Two police constables on their beat in the early hours of a Sunday morning heard loud arguing, cursing and swearing emanating from within particular premises. One hour later, they returned to hear the commotion still continuing. They could distinctly hear at a distance of some 30 yards from the premises that a particular individual was being denounced. It was at that point that they intervened. There obviously was disturbance of the peace one would have expected to reign at that hour (3–4 am) of the Sabbath in the streets of Stranraer. But, since no one was proved to have been within earshot of the premises, apart from the two police constables, had the author of the commotion been rightly convicted of breach of the peace? That was the question put to the High Court. The court had no doubt that he had.

2.17   Of the two opinions delivered, that of Lord Justice-Clerk Macdonald is the more general. From the common parts of the two versions of his speech, the following definition can be deduced: breach of the peace consists of proven (or admitted) conduct on the part of the accused from which the court can reasonably infer, in all the relevant circumstances, that alarm was likely to have been created in the minds of the lieges — ie alarm in the sense of fear for their personal safety, or alarm in the sense of a belief that the conduct in question was causing, or that continuance of that conduct would cause real (or perhaps serious) disturbance of the standing peace of the *locus* and its immediate surroundings. (The 'lieges' here were to be understood either as 'ordinary people' (16 R (J) at 94) or as 'sober and reasonably minded people' (2 White at 281).) What was not made clear in this definition was whether the 'lieges' might include the two constables who appeared as the only witnesses in the case. The view can be taken that those police officers would hardly have been alarmed for themselves by behaviour of the sort featured in the case, but that they might well have been of the persuasion that continuance of that behaviour would have resulted in real disturbance of the peace of that part of Stranraer. Equally, the Lord Justice-Clerk may have taken the view that the evidence of the police was simply factual evidence from which the court might make the required inference in relation to ordinary members of the public and their mental state — had such members of the public actually been present along with the two constables. Was the inference to be made, therefore, in relation to the likely reaction of those who did hear the shouting, cursing and swearing, or in relation to those who might have heard it if they had been present? This question is not answered. (To some extent, it now has been answered — see **2.23**, below.) But the whole of Lord Justice-Clerk Macdonald's definition (in terms of the Humean requirements of disturbance and alarm — see **1.15**, above) is thrown into some confusion by his remark that 'sober and reasonably minded people might be seriously *annoyed* by a disturbance such as is set forth in this case'. This suggests that at least in the instant case, it would have been enough to infer 'annoyance' on the part of the lieges, although annoyance is a significantly weaker mental state than one of alarm (see OED for definitions). The word 'annoyed' appears, however, only in the 2 White version of his speech (at p 281), and it would have been possible to ignore it as (say) an editorial aberration. (That it has not subsequently been ignored has resulted in considerable widening of the concept of the offence.)

2.18   This definition proffered by the Lord Justice-Clerk is, therefore, perfectly general in its terms and emphasises that courts should focus not so much upon the conduct of the accused as upon the effect, or likely effect, of that conduct on the minds of the public. Although there clearly must be conduct which amounts, or is capable of amounting, to some sort of disturbance, it must also cause, or be likely to cause, alarm. The *locus* will, therefore, be of some importance as will the circumstances; and the whole issue is governed by the test of reasonableness. This is possibly a workable definition (which might have been acquiesced in by Hume).

2.19   Lord McLaren delivered the second opinion in *Ferguson v Carnochan*. His is a singularly confusing opinion, made rather more difficult by the existence of the two versions of it. In so far as any general definition is proffered at all, it lies in this, that 'Breach of the peace means a breach of public order and decorum . . .'. This seems to concentrate on the conduct involved. But the 'definition' continues in terms '. . . causing disturbance and alarm to members of the public' (2 White at 282), or, '. . . accompanied always by the qualification that it is to the alarm and annoyance of the public' (16 R (J) at 94). The common feature of these extensions is that the type of breach he refers to should 'cause' or 'be to' the alarm of the public; but it is uncertain whether he had in mind actual alarm or just the likelihood of it in the circumstances. In addition, no attempt is made to explain what is meant by 'decorum'. (Presumably, it carries its ordinary meaning of decency or propriety.) The remainder of Lord McLaren's speech (see Appendix) is concerned with specific instances which may or may not amount to breaches of the peace, amongst which is considered 'brawling ... where offensive language is used', that being the particular scenario in *Ferguson v Carnochan* itself. From the differing nature of the two versions of his speech, all that can be deduced here is that such conduct is a breach of public order and decorum and that it will also amount to a breach of the peace if those who hear it are alarmed for their personal safety or if the court (?) takes the view that it would cause reasonable fear (possibly, 16 R (J) at 94, in the minds of those who actually hear it) that mischief may result to the culprit or others (or possibly, 16 R (J) at 94, just to the public peace itself). It is very difficult to make sense of any of this, and consequently very difficult to draw anything of general value from the whole speech. The fact that later courts have drawn extensively on selected parts of one or other of the versions of Lord McLaren's opinion is quite astonishing (as is the fact that in the case itself, Lord Rutherfurd-Clark simply concurred). Nevertheless, it has been stated with considerable *de facto* justification that this case is widely regarded as forming the basis of the modern law (see JSF 'Breach of the Peace' 78 (1962) Sc Law Rev 73).

2.20 In particular, much use was made of *Ferguson v Carnochan* in the leading case of *Raffaelli v Heatly* (1949 SLT 284), where the accused was convicted of a charge that 'about 11.50 pm on 29th September 1948 [in St Leonard's Hill, Edinburgh, he] did conduct [himself] in a disorderly manner, peer in at a lighted window of the dwelling house at number 10 there, put residents in said street in a state of fear and alarm, and commit a breach of the peace'. Both counsel at the subsequent appeal founded on *Ferguson v Carnochan*, as did Lord Mackay (in a typically rambling but interesting speech). The definition of breach of the peace, however, given out by Lord Justice-Clerk Thomson in this case has been very influential and has been quoted with approval on many occasions by the High Court (see, eg, *Butcher v Jessop* 1989 SCCR 119 at 130D, per Lord Justice-Clerk Ross). The famous words are these: '[W]here something is done in breach of public order or decorum which might reasonably be expected to lead to the lieges being alarmed or upset or tempted to make reprisals at their own hand, the circumstances are such as to amount to a breach of the peace' (1949 SLT at 285). The Lord Justice-Clerk cited no authority for this wide-ranging view of the crime, but it is obvious that the first part is borrowed from Lord McLaren (in *Ferguson v Carnochan*) with the subtle alteration of 'or' as the relevant conjuction between 'public order' and 'decorum'. (Lord Mackay at 286 noted that Lord McLaren had referred to 'public order and decorum', but opined that he could not possibly have meant that; he must have intended to refer to public order or decorum — although none of the printed versions of Lord McLaren's opinion gives any basis for that view.) That amendment, since decorum means decent or proper conduct, enabled the court to conclude that Raffaelli's 'peeping tom' activities were indecorous (there being, as Lord Mackay supposed at 286, a faint sexual flavour to peering through a three-quarter inch gap between drawn curtains into a lighted living room which happened to contain a bed). It will be noted that the Lord Justice-Clerk's words continue to stress that the required effect of the conduct on the minds of the lieges may be treated as a matter of reasonable inference from the circumstances. The required effect, then, need not actually be experienced by anyone. But that effect is not confined to alarm (as, say, defined by the Lord Justice-Clerk in *Ferguson v Carnochan*). It may now amount to 'upset' only (*quaere* if that differs from 'annoyance'); or more narrowly, it may simply amount to a temptation to make reprisals against the author of the 'breach of public order or decorum'. Such temptation would seem to result from treating the accused's conduct as provocative — a view as old as Blackstone and probably espoused by Hume (see **1.04**, above). Thus in *MacNeill v Robertson* (1982 SCCR 468), Sheriff Scott declared that breach of the peace 'consists of conduct which may reasonably be expected to cause any person to be alarmed, upset or annoyed or to provoke a disturbance of the peace' (at p 469). In this, his views are remarkably similar to those of Lord Dunpark in *Wilson v Brown* (1982 SCCR 49) where (at p 51) the following appears: 'It is well settled that a test which may be applied in charges of breach of the peace is whether the proved conduct may reasonably be expected to cause any person to be alarmed, upset or annoyed or to provoke a disturbance of the peace. Positive evidence of actual alarm, upset, annoyance or disturbance created by reprisal is not a prerequisite of conviction . . . .' (It will be noted that Lord Dunpark did not suggest that this was the only test.)

2.21   The various tests outlined above are all in current use by the courts. The tests of Lord Justice-Clerk Macdonald in *Ferguson v Carnochan* and Lord Justice-Clerk Thomson in *Raffaelli v Heatly* were, for example, both quoted with approval by Lord Justice-Clerk Ross in the leading modern case of *Butcher v Jessop* (1989 SCCR 119 at 130B and D); and Lord Dunpark's test in *Wilson v Brown* was, for example, quoted with approval by Lord Justice-Clerk Ross in *Norris v McLeod* (1988 SCCR 572 at 575). It may be thought that these are not unreasonable tests, and they certainly are applied in the daily business of modern courts. But the extension from 'alarm' on the one hand to 'annoyance' and 'upset' on the other mirrors the extension of breach of the peace to the less-sinister, nuisance-value conduct which was formerly the province of minor police offences.

2.22 Where such alarm, annoyance or upset cannot be shown to exist in actuality and must be inferred as likely to follow from the conduct (and circumstances), Lord Justice-General Clyde (in *Young v Heatly* 1959 JC 66 at 70) said this: 'I consider that a very special case requires to be made out by the prosecution if a conviction for breach of the peace is to follow in the absence of ... evidence of alarm or annoyance. For then the nature of the conduct giving rise to the offence must be so flagrant as to entitle the court to draw the necessary inference from the conduct itself.' In practice, little use has been found for this caveat; and courts have apparently experienced little difficulty in drawing the 'necessary inference' in cases which are deemed to require it.

A result crime

2.23 From the general definitions considered above, it is plain that (following Gordon's useful analysis — see *Gordon*, 3-05) breach of the peace is a 'result crime'. There must, of course, be proven (or admitted) conduct on the part of the accused. But that will not suffice for conviction unless there is a result of a particular kind. The fact that the result may be inferred does not disturb this conclusion; from the point of view of its *actus reus*, the crime is a 'result' one. Because the types of conduct which the courts have found sufficient for this crime are of a very varied nature, these will be considered separately (see III, below). Also, since the required result is dependent upon the sort of conduct involved, it is thought that a single definition of breach of the peace is impractical. It is possible, however, that two general statements may encapsulate the modern view of the *actus reus* of the crime: viz. (1) breach of the peace consists of proven or admitted conduct on the part of the accused where there is also evidence that that conduct caused, or if allowed to continue would reasonably in all the circumstances have been likely to cause, by way of provocation of others or otherwise, real [meaning 'significant'] disturbance of the standing peace of the immediate and surrounding area where the conduct occurred; and, (2) breach of the peace also consists of proven or admitted conduct on the part of the accused from which, in all the circumstances, a court can reasonably infer that any reasonable person might be alarmed, upset, annoyed or suffer any other similar mental trauma as a result. (It should be noted here that it has now been decided that police constables are included amongst persons who might reasonably be upset or annoyed by conduct consisting of swearing and verbal abuse — *Norris v McLeod* 1988 SCCR 572; *Saltman v Allan* 1988 SCCR 640; *McMillan v Normand* 1989 SCCR 269. There is also no reason to suppose that they might not experience alarm in appropriate circumstances — cf *DPP v Orum* [1989] 1 WLR 88.)

Mens rea

2.24   None of the general definitions of breach of the peace mentions the matter of dole. Yet this is a common law offence and the general principle of the common law in Scotland is believed to be that *actus non facit reum nisi mens sit rea* (*Gordon*, 7-01). Unfortunately, few cases on breach of the peace have ever raised the matter of *mens rea*. Of the few where it has been discussed, the view has sometimes been taken that *mens rea* is required; but if that is so, it is uncertain what form *mens rea* should take here, although (in the usual Scottish manner) it is certain that it may be inferred from the facts.

2.25   The latest case which is relevant here is *Butcher v Jessop* (1989 SCCR 119). During a football match, it was found that the goalkeeper for one team had struck with his elbow the chin of a player from the opposing team, seized him by the throat, and pushed him to the ground. In this, the goalkeeper had been assisted by his own team captain who approached the unfortunate player and struck him in the chest. (The whole incident lasted a mere seven seconds, but caused a certain amount of unrest amongst sections of the 43,000-strong crowd.) These facts were important since they suggested that the offences committed might have been assaults and might have been charged as such. In fact, all charges against the accused were of the form that while participating in a football match, they did conduct themselves in a disorderly manner and commit a breach of the peace. The flavour of assault, however, undoubtedly seasoned the attitude of the sheriff to the question of dole. It was strongly maintained before him (and indeed again before the Appeal Court) that the accused lacked the *mens rea* necessary for the crime. It was argued that they had simply been playing a game and were exhibiting the exuberance to be expected as incidental thereto and for which the rules catered. Sheriff McKay (at 125E) simply stated that there was abundant evidence before him from which *mens rea* could be inferred, and that he would so infer it (at 125F). This means that he accepted that breach of the peace required *mens rea*, although regrettably the form it required to take was not disclosed. But, as the learned sheriff considered that the accused had been guilty of assaults which were also breaches of the peace (at 122G–123A), he may have been thinking of the 'evil intent to injure' which assaults are said to require (*Smart v HM Advocate* 1975

JC 30). When the players' appeals against conviction came to be heard, Lord Justice-Clerk Ross (Lord Allanbridge concurring) ruled that it had been wrong to make any finding of assault, since assault had been no part of the Crown's case (at 129B –C). He then turned to the matter of dole, and ruled (at 130A–B) that Gordon's view of the matter (at 41-09) was correct, viz.: '[I]t is not necessary to show that the accused intended to provoke a disturbance, it is enough that his conduct was such that the court regarded it as objectively calculated to do so.' On the assumption that 'calculated' there means 'likely' (cf **2.106**, below) it is difficult to resist the inference that *mens rea* in the form of intention to create a particular result is not a requirement of breach of the peace (or, at least, not a requirement of this particular form of the crime). Whilst it is true that Lord Murray's opinion insists on finding some basis in the facts for 'criminal intent' (at 136c), it is also true that his opinion is a dissenting one. (He was also clearly thinking of the offences as ones involving the essentials of assault — see 136D–E.)

2.26 The majority view in *Butcher v Jessop* (1989 SCCR 119) receives implied support from a number of decisions. For example, in *Palazzo v Copeland* (1976 JC 52), the accused discharged a shotgun into the air with the sole intention of bringing an existing disturbance of the peace to an end. The Appeal Court accepted that that was so, but regarded it simply as his motive (and thus irrelevant). What the court regarded as truly significant was that his conduct was objectively 'calculated' (ie 'likely') to cause alarm to the public (when all the circumstances were taken into account), and that that was all that was necessary for conviction. (It ought to be said, however, that he clearly did intend to cause alarm — viz. to the youths who were causing a fracas in the street adjacent to his house — and that such alarm was caused.) Likewise in *Dougall v Dykes* (1861) 4 Irv 101, a conviction for breach of the peace was upheld by the High Court even though the original charge had libelled 'malice' which the jury had expressly negatived. Both Lord Neaves (at 105) and Lord Justice-Clerk Inglis (at 106) confirmed that the conduct was 'calculated' (in the sense of 'likely') to produce disturbance, and that that was entirely sufficient. Also, in *Deakin v Milne* (1882) 5 Coup 174, the High Court affirmed that the Salvation Army may have had the best of intentions in marching in noisy procession through the streets of Arbroath, but that lack of intent to effect disturbance was not a relevant consideration. What really mattered was the preservation of order and peace in the burgh in question. (Again, however, it should be noted that the accused did know that their processions had in the recent past caused disturbances by provoking their opponents to violent counter-demonstrations.)

2.27   All of the cases so far mentioned in this section can, however, be reconciled with the view that breach of the peace requires reckless-ness or carelessness. In each of them, it can be shown that at the very least, the accused were careless as to the possibility of disturbance as a result of his or their conduct — a suggestion for the *mens rea* of the crime made in an article contributed to the Scots Law Times in 1959 ('Breach of the Peace', 1959 SLT (News) 229), and given some credence in *Carmichael v Boyle* (1985 SLT 399). Boyle in that case was charged with a number of offences including assault and breach of the peace. He was eventually acquitted of them all by Sheriff Boyle on the basis that it had not been proved that he had the necessary *mens rea*. As the accused, a diabetic, had been suffering from hypoglycaemia at the material times, this was quite plausible. But what was the *mens rea* which he lacked? If intention was required, then Sheriff Boyle was confident that his mental state might well have precluded its form-ation; again, if recklessness was required, then he probably could not, because of his lack of intelligence, have been able to foresee that neglecting his diabetic regime would have resulted in aggressive, unpredictable and uncontrollable conduct. The learned sheriff con-ceded that *mens rea* in Scots criminal law was generally satisfied as a matter of inference from the accused's conduct; but in the peculiar circumstances of this case, he was satisfied that that inference could not be drawn. On a subsequent appeal by the prosecutor, the High Court (Lord Justice-Clerk Wheatley, Lords Robertson and Jauncey) affirmed that *mens rea* was a matter of inference from the proven conduct — and that the necessary inference(s) must be drawn here. Thus, the sheriff was ordered to convict.

2.28   It is difficult to draw any firm conclusions from the case of *Carmichael v Boyle* (see **2.27**, above). *Ex facie*, it seems to accept that breach of the peace requires *mens rea*. Once again, however, assault was involved; and it may be that the Appeal Court was addressing itself primarily to that. The case is also complicated in that it would have involved (had the sheriff's decision stood) substantial dilution of the position taken in *HM Advocate v Cunningham* (1963 JC 80) — a result which the court was obviously most anxious to avoid (see **2.32–2.35**, below). In any event, even if there is some authority here for breach of the peace's requiring *mens rea*, it is completely uncertain what form that *mens rea* should take.

2.29   If intention (for example, intention to create a disturbance) was what was being required, that would seem inconsistent with the cases discussed above (at **2.25** to **2.26**). If recklessness was what the sheriff and the Appeal Court had in mind, this in Scotland is certainly simple enough to prove. The proof is objective (*pace* the apparent contrary view taken by Sheriff Boyle — see **2.27**, above), and the standard formula for recklessness *can* be adapted to suit many instances of breach of the peace. The standard objective formula was laid down in *Allan v Patterson* (1980 SLT 77 at 80) and would thus read *mutatis mutandis*:

'Judges and juries will readily understand, and juries might well be reminded, that before they can apply the adverb "recklessly" to the [conduct] in question they must find that it fell far below the standard of [conduct] expected of the [ordinary, decent and law-abiding citizen] and that it occurred either in the face of obvious and material dangers [of disturbance or annoyance or upset] which were or should have been observed, appreciated and guarded against, or in circumstances which showed a complete disregard for any potential dangers [of disturbance or annoyance or upset] which might result from the way in which the [accused was conducting himself].'

This, however, is not only exceedingly clumsy but is probably too exacting and subtle for the practicalities of the offence. No reported case on breach of the peace shows such a test being used, although some can be explained (*ex post facto*) by reference to it (eg *Butcher v Jessop* 1989 SCCR 119, **2.25**, above; and *Deakin v Milne* (1882) 5 Coup 174, **2.26**, above). Nevertheless, it is thought that if *mens rea* is required, it must relate to something short of intention or recklessness.

2.30   If carelessness as to the likelihood of disturbance (or alarm or whatever) is what really has to be inferred, it would seem that positive steps taken by the accused to avoid the possibility of disturbance should prevent such an inference being drawn. But as has been pointed out ('Breach of the Peace', 1959 SLT (News) 229 at 232), in *Young v Heatly* (1959 JC 66) the efforts of the accused to make his remarks in total privacy were ignored; and further, in *Shannon v Skeen* ((1977) SCCR Supp 180), where the accused persisted in following a woman (who was collecting money from vending machines) and totally ignored the obvious distress and alarm they were causing her, the Appeal Court quashed their convictions for breach of the peace, apparently on the ground that their motive was not a criminal one. (They were private detectives hired by a prospective purchaser of the vending machine business to find out how often the machines themselves were attended to.)

2.31   The role which *mens rea* plays and the form (if any) which it takes in breach of the peace remain, therefore, mysterious. Given the want of cogent authority on this issue, it would be better to assume that no particular form of dole is required, and that no realistic defence can be mounted on the basis that one's client lacked *mens rea* (see *Ralston v HM Advocate* 1988 SCCR 590).

Voluntariness of conduct

2.32 The foregoing discussion of *mens rea* in relation to breach of the peace (see **2.24** to **2.31**) concerned the result which is required for conviction. There is also arguably a form of *mens rea* relative to the conduct which causes that result, though it is more common to refer to such form as 'voluntariness' or 'deliberateness'. Must, therefore, the relevant conduct be deliberate or voluntary before conviction can follow?

2.33 Some support for 'deliberateness' being required appears from part of Lord Justice-Clerk Ross's opinion (with which Lord Allanbridge agreed) in *Butcher v Jessop* (1989 SCCR 119) where it was said (at 130E):

'Applying that test [ie of Lord Justice-Clerk Thomson in *Raffaelli v Heatly* 1949 SLT 284 at 285, see **2.20**, above], what the sheriff had to do in the present case was to determine whether the actings complained of were deliberate, and, if so, whether they amounted to breach of the peace as so defined.'

Lord Murray (dissenting) also said as much in the same case, viz. (at 134B): 'First, it must be proved beyond reasonable doubt that conduct which is intended is disorderly . . .' But when consideration is given to the context in respect of which these remarks were made (ie that the accused were players in a game of football), it is suggested that their Lordships simply meant that it should be found as a matter of fact that the conduct was not, or did not look accidental. The background of 'assault' must also be borne in mind. Non-deliberate actions which caused injury could never be considered assaults. Such actions would not fulfil Macdonald's definition of assault in terms of an attack on the person of another (*Macdonald*, p 115) — a definition which has been judicially approved on many occasions (eg *Smart v HM Advocate* 1975 SLT 65 at 66). In any event, accident is also a recognised defence in Scots criminal law (eg *Mackenzie v HM Advocate* 1983 SLT 220); and, therefore, the above suggested interpretation is at least consistent with established law.

2.34 It would not, however, be consistent with established law to read the above (**2.33**) references to 'deliberate' or 'intentional' conduct as if a general finding of 'voluntariness' was now being required. If that were so, then it would surely enable an accused person to argue that his conduct was involuntary because of some 'mental or pathological condition short of insanity' from which he was suffering at the time. But such an argument was expressly excluded many years ago in the course of a High Court ruling (*HM Advocate v Cunningham* 1963 JC 80) which has been recently declared to suffer no exceptions (*Carmichael v Boyle* 1985 SLT 399 — a case which did involve a submission of involuntariness due to hypoglycaemia in answer to *inter alia* a charge of breach of the peace).

2.35   It must follow, therefore, that breach of the peace does not form an exception to the general rule. The conduct of the accused will be assumed to be voluntary or deliberate unless it is shown to be accidental or indulged in by one who meets the Scottish test for insanity as set out in *HM Advocate v Kidd* 1960 JC 61 and *Brennan v HM Advocate* 1977 SLT 151 (but cf *Ralston v HM Advocate* 1988 SCCR 590).

Conduct need not be in public

2.36   There is no strong evidence that Hume saw breaches of the peace as necessarily involving conduct indulged in in a public place (see **1.16**, above). It is true, however, that he does refer to breaches of the public peace (see **1.03**, above) and to disturbances of the neighbourhood; and it is also true that disturbance is more likely to exist in public places where people are obviously wont (and entitled) to be. But in modern law, no actual disturbance or alarm (or annoyance or upset or whatever) need ever be shown to justify conviction. All that is really necessary is evidence of conduct from which a court can reasonably infer that disturbance of the standing peace of the immediate and surrounding area did or would occur, or that any reasonable person might be alarmed, upset, annoyed (or whatever) by it (see **2.23**, above). A large variety of *loci* can, therefore, be accommodated by breach of the peace, as the reported cases amply demonstrate. What seems to be required is that the conduct takes place where there are persons (affected by it) present or takes immediate and direct effect where persons could reasonably be expected to be. Thus, there is no necessary restriction to a public place. On the other hand, it would be patently absurd to suggest that 'a breach of the peace can be committed anywhere, even in a locked sound-proof windowless room on a desert island, provided the court is prepared to say that had it taken place in public it would have been likely to lead to an actual breach of the peace' ('Breach of the Peace', 1959 SLT (News) 229 at 232). One cannot commit this offence in the absence of other people or in relation to a place where the presence of other people cannot reasonably be anticipated. Thus, the presence of others must usually be anticipated in the public streets, roads and lanes of a built-up area, or indeed in any place to which (and while) the public has unrestricted access (as, for example, 'public place' is defined in the Civic Government (Scotland) Act 1982, s 133) or are permitted to have access, on payment or otherwise (again following by way of example the 1982 Act, s 50(6)(a)).

2.37 Nothing is more common than breach of the peace charges which specify the *locus* as the public streets of a town. Thus, in *Logan v Jessop* (1987 SCCR 604), the complaint read: 'On 20th February 1986, in Westray Circus, Glasgow, near Westray Street, you did conduct yourself in a disorderly manner, shout, swear and commit a breach of the peace.' It would be pointless to cite further such examples. Scarcely less common are *loci* of the description that the public are permitted access to them. In reported cases, these have included municipal buildings maintained for the benefit of the public (eg Dundee Swimming Pool and Leisure Complex — *Deasley v Hogg* 1976 SLT (Notes) 7); sports stadia whether in public ownership or not (eg Ibrox Stadium — *Butcher v Jessop* 1989 SCCR 119); courts of law and their precincts (eg Inverness Sheriff Court — *Dyce v Aitchison* 1985 SCCR 184); police stations (eg Cumbernauld police office — *Carmichael v Monaghan* 1986 SCCR 598); public houses, shops or their equivalents (eg a smithy — *James Ainslie* (1842) 1 Broun 25, charge (4) *quoad* breach of the peace); public conveyances (eg a railway train compartment — *Hackston v Millar* (1906) 5 Adam 37; or a bus — *McLean v McNaughton* 1984 SCCR 319); public lavatories (eg *Hay v Wither* 1988 SCCR 334, charge (1)); places where public meetings are being held (eg *Sleigh & Russell v Moxey* (1850) J Shaw 369); and, places where religious services or meetings are in progress (eg *Hugh Fraser* (1839) 2 Swin 436; *Hendry v Ferguson* (1883) 5 Coup 278).

2.38 With respect to non-public places such as private dwelling houses conduct may cause disturbance or alarm (or upset or annoyance) to persons actually within or on such premises along with the accused, or may be of such proportion in the circumstances as to have immediate and direct effect on individuals (real or reasonably to be anticipated) beyond the confines of such premises.

2.39 Persons with the accused in a non-public place and affected by his conduct may, and indeed will very likely, be members of his own family. In *Avery v Hilson* ((1906) 5 Adam 56), for example, a complaint, which specified that Avery in his own dwelling house conducted himself in a riotous and disorderly manner and committed a breach of the peace by going about cursing, swearing and threatening to shoot his wife with a gun he had in his hand at the time, was received without objection. (Nor could it have been objected to on the basis of the *locus* specified.) Similarly, in *Carmichael v Boyle* (1985 SCCR 58), the accused was (*inter alia*) charged with breach of the peace by virtue of his aggressive conduct in his mother's house, where his mother, his mistress and police officers were present. There is no requirement, however, that persons other than police officers should be present, although the police would presumably require to be there in the execution of their duty — as they were in *Saltman v Allan* (1989 SLT 262), a case which concerned swearing and aggressive conduct towards the police in the private access road to a farm. It must, it is thought, be the case that private premises would include not only buildings (as in *McMillan v Normand* 1989 SCCR 269) and access roads but also private vehicles and boats. (Thus, for example, in *McNaughton v McPherson* 1980 SLT (Notes) 97, one of the charges brought against the four accused was breach of the peace committed on board a yacht berthed in Rothesay harbour; but the report of the case is meagre, and the precise circumstances unclear.

2.40 Even if there is no-one with the accused in or on private premises who is himself alarmed, conduct within such premises may have a wider effect giving rise to a charge of breach of the peace. In *Ferguson v Carnochan* ((1889) 2 White 278), for example, the accused was shouting, cursing and swearing and making 'a great noise and disturbance' inside his own premises in the presence of his wife and another (neither of whom having been apparently perturbed by his conduct). Such was the volume of his shouts and imprecations, however, that they could be heard outside in the public street and were so heard by two constables on patrol. It was submitted on his behalf, in the course of an appeal against conviction for breach of the peace, that the conviction was incompetent since the conduct took place in private and there was no firm evidence that anyone had been disturbed by it. Both these arguments were struck down by the court. In particular, the court willingly felt itself bound by the decision in *Matthews & Rodden v Linton* ((1860) 3 Irv 570) to hold that a breach of the peace could be committed in a private house. There is little doubt, however, that the reason for the court's decision was the direct and immediate effect which the conduct had outside the house — viz. that it could be heard in the public streets of Stranraer and would have caused disturbance or alarm to any reasonable person there. (There is nothing in the somewhat sparse report of *Matthews & Rodden v Linton* expressly to suggest that that was also the rationale of the decision there. But the conduct was more serious, extending to actual fighting, and the charge narrated that the lieges *were* annoyed and disturbed by it.) A clearer illustration perhaps emerges from *Liszewski v Thomson* (1942 SLT 147) where three Scottish women and three Polish soldiers were convicted of breach of the peace in that they had been shouting, cursing and swearing *inter se* within a private house. But it was specifically found that the shouts and bad language had been heard by passers-by outside, and that a crowd had gathered — all at between 1 and 2 am during an air-raid alarm. That conduct inside private premises, therefore, had a direct and immediate effect on persons outside. It should not be thought, however, that relevant conduct is restricted to sound — verbal or otherwise. What can be seen (or perhaps smelled?) taking place in or on private premises is equally capable of affecting persons outside. An illustration of this will be found in *Donaghy v Tudhope* (1985 SCCR 118), where four protestors entered a building site, climbed two tower cranes there and unfurled protest-banners. They shouted and gesticulated from the cranes at passers-by to attract attention to their protest — thereby causing alarm to some and annoyance to others (in particular to the building site employees whose efforts to work during the protest were obviously frustrated).

2.41   In each of the illustrations so far discussed (at **2.40**, above), the wider effect of the conduct in or on private premises was (or would by inference have been) direct and fairly immediate. It is thought that this is a requirement of breach of the peace in general — viz. that the conduct should create immediate, direct disturbance or annoyance (or any other of the recognised mental states), or should be found in the circumstances reasonably capable of doing so (if, for example, it was allowed to continue — cf *Thompson v MacPhail* 1989 SCCR 266). There is, however, one (much criticised) case decision which appears to cast doubts on that requirement of immediacy and directness. In *Young v Heatly* (1959 JC 66), a depute headmaster of a technical college made certain remarks to three male students in the private confines of his own room. Each student was spoken to on his own and each was either 16 or 17 years of age. The remarks related to the youths' (and the headmaster's) masturbatory and homosexual experiences. There was no finding in fact (by the magistrate in the Burgh Court of Edinburgh, as it then was) that any of the students was alarmed or annoyed (although that seems an extremely surprising if not suspicious omission, given what had been said). At the end of the day, the accused was convicted on four counts of breach of the peace (of the 'conduct himself in a disorderly manner' type — see **2.01** to **2.04**, above). His appeal against conviction was unsuccessful. Unfortunately, the reason for his conviction is unclear. It can certainly be accepted on authority that it would not have been a good reason *per se* for quashing his conviction that the conduct complained of had taken place in private. The problem is that breach of the peace is a result crime (**2.23**, above); and the Appeal Court here did not explain how one or other of the requisite results for breach of the peace had been arrived at. Lord Russell in fact declared that he had not found the issues raised in the case 'free from difficulty' (p 71); but nevertheless agreed (as did Lord Carmont) with Lord Justice-General Clyde that the conviction should stand. It appears to have been accepted by the court that the youths were not themselves alarmed or annoyed by the accused's behaviour. But actual alarm or annoyance has never been thought of as essential. Ultimately, the decision in *Young v Heatly* was simply made on the peculiar facts and circumstances of the case (as several commentators have pointed out — viz. *Gordon* at 41-08; the learned but anonymous author of 'Breach of the Peace', 1959 SLT (News) 229 at 232); but the question remains whether it can be reconciled with the modern view of breach of the peace where the behaviour in question occurs in private.

2.42   It would be possible to consider the youths, the addressees of the remarks, as neutral observers of the conduct, playing a role similar to that often played by police witnesses. Their combined evidence (on application of the 'Moorov' principle — see *Moorov v HM Advocate* 1930 JC 68) would simply provide the court with the facts and circumstances from which a reasonable inference might be made that any reasonable person would have been alarmed or annoyed (or whatever) by the accused's conduct. This would enable the privacy of the *locus* virtually to be ignored. It might further have the strange consequence of labelling the youths as other than reasonable persons, but is not wholly untenable. Alternatively (although this seems much distant from Lord Justice-General Clyde's actual opinion), it could be argued that whilst the youths were not alarmed (or annoyed or whatever) for their own parts, it was a reasonable inference that they might have been alarmed that their parents or friends would be alarmed, annoyed or perhaps provoked into making reprisals at their own hands, were a report of what had taken place to come to their ears. This argument would not, however, square the decision with the cases considered at **2.40**, above. It does admittedly consider the privacy of the occasion and, in the absence of actual alarm (etc), finds a wider, even 'public' effect without which there would be no breach of the peace. But that wider effect could not reasonably be said to follow directly and immediately from the conduct. Indeed it would not follow from *the conduct* at all, but from a later report of it (cf *Turner v Kennedy* (1972) SCCR Supp 30, where copies of a pamphlet handed out in the street to school pupils were at once taken home by some of those pupils and handed to their parents). The conduct itself (to which only the youths could speak) might long have ceased; and further, their speaking of it to others would be a matter entirely at their discretion. It is thought that an inference of alarm in relation to (eg) possible reprisals at such a remove from the conduct in question (and when it could only be prompted by a report anent that conduct) would not be a reasonable one, and even more unreasonable when the original conduct had occurred in a private place under such circumstances as pertained in *Young v Heatly*. (Lest it be thought that *Raffaelli v Heatly* (1949 JC 101) gives some support to the drawing of such an inference, it should be recalled that Mrs Price in that case *was* alarmed in fact, the conduct was not in private, there were several eye witnesses, and the remarks of Lord Justice-General Thomson and Lord Mackay *quoad* Mrs Price's reasons for not informing her husband (ie that he might be tempted to take the law into his own hands) were really *obiter*.)

2.43   In truth *Young v Heatly* is not a case which casts doubts on the necessity of finding a wider effect of the nature referred to at **2.41**, above, where the conduct complained of occurs in private and no actual alarm or annoyance (or whatever) can be demonstrated. It is indeed a case which depends on its own facts and circumstances. With hindsight, Young's conduct should have been prosecuted (if at all) as shamelessly indecent conduct (see *Watt v Annan* 1978 SLT 198, and the account of that offence given by Lord Cameron at 201).

2.44   It is not then the private or public nature of the *locus* which really decides whether breach of the peace is an appropriate charge or not. What counts is whether reasonable persons are alarmed or annoyed (or whatever) in fact, or whether it is likely that they reasonably would be. If the accused's conduct occurs in such a place and in such circumstances that it cannot reasonably have any wider, direct and immediate effect on other persons (see, for example, the facts found in *Thompson v MacPhail* 1989 SCCR 266), then it should not be considered as a breach of the peace (although it may amount to some other offence). The *locus* then is simply one of the circumstances of which a court must take note. An unbearably noisy celebration or party in one flat of an apartment block may, for example, have no wider effect than the upstairs, downstairs or adjacent private apartment; but that would be sufficient if a complaint of annoyance were made, or perhaps, in the absence of firm complaint, if the surrounding apartments were in fact occupied. It could not be a defence that the noise was not audible in the streets outside; although if the noise *was* so audible (as in *Ferguson v Carnochan* (1889) 2 White 278), it would be easier to draw an inference of annoyance since the public streets may well have people in them at any hour of the day or night.

Art and part guilt of breach of the peace

2.45   There is no reason why a person who does not himself take part in conduct amounting to breach of the peace should not be guilty of that offence art and part. It is always to be assumed in any event that a person is charged in that capacity or as actor (Criminal Procedure (Scotland) Act 1975, s 312(d)). The point was well underlined by Sheriff Scott in *MacNeill v Robertson* (1982 SCCR 468) where he said (at 469):

'[R]esponsibility for the acts of others only arises if it is proved affirmatively that there was a common plan and that the accused was a party to the common plan. I am satisfied that a person may be guilty of breach of the peace, art and part, in accordance with that basic principle.'

The common plan would have to involve an intention that the acts amounting to breach-of-the-peace-conduct should be carried out; but that need not, of course, amount to knowledge (still less intention) that what was to be done should amount to a breach of the peace. In *MacNeill v Robertson*, two breach of the peace charges were brought against a total of sixteen persons. The first charge (which varied from the second only in matters of detail) alleged: '. . . you . . . did form part of a disorderly crowd, members of which did shout, swear, challenge others to fight, brandish sticks, bars and broken bottles, beat on the roof of a motor vehicle, and commit a breach of the peace.' The learned sheriff *ex proprio motu* questioned the relevancy of the charges since they did not amount to mobbing (there being no assertion of any common purpose) and could not amount to art and part guilt (there being no assertion in his view of any common plan to which the accused had been party). It will be noted that the charges (which were identical in this respect) did not suggest that the accused themselves had indulged in any of the activities listed. It was simply asserted that they had been part of a crowd, some members of which had behaved in those fashions. Although Sheriff Scott's dismissal of the charges on the grounds of their irrelevancy was challenged on appeal, the High Court simply dismissed the Crown's appeal without delivering any opinions. It seems to follow from that that Sheriff Scott's views on art and part guilt of breach of the peace had been endorsed; and this indeed is confirmed by the decision of the Appeal Court in *Winnik v Allan* (1986 SCCR 35). There, the court agreed that it had been right to find the accused guilty of breach of the peace by participation. He had been charged:

'[Y]ou did form part of a crowd of noisy and disorderly persons who shouted and swore and tore down a stone boundary wall and threw missiles at [Blinkbonny] colliery buildings . . . and did commit a breach of the peace.'

Although it had not been proved that the accused himself had shouted, sworn, or torn down or thrown anything, he had arrived at the colliery as part of a group of forty or fifty 'flying pickets' whose plan was plainly to picket the mine and to obstruct the egress and ingress of persons thereto. Since he had made no attempt to dissociate himself prior to the complained-of conduct of those he was with, the sheriff inferred that his presence there was not susceptible of an innocent explanation, and that he must be guilty art and part. He had been a party to the common plan to do what had been done, and that was sufficient for conviction. The Appeal Court agreed that that inference had been correctly drawn and that the decision to convict had been right.

2.46   It remains for consideration to what extent reporters, television crews and other media persons, who learn of a plan such as that found in *Winnik v Allan* (1986 SCCR 35), would be guilty of breach of the peace art and part if they remained whilst such a plan was executed and by their presence gave (additional?) impetus to its implementation (or, indeed, development). No doubt such persons would argue that their roles were truly neutral ones. But in principle, in appropriate circumstances, there is no reason why they might not face charges.

Attempt

2.47   Although it is plausible to think in terms of a conspiracy or an incitement to commit a breach of the peace, the matter of an attempt to commit one poses some difficulty. The modern definitions of the offence (see **2.15** to **2.22**, above) are conceived in terms of what is likely to happen (as well as what has happened) as a result of the accused's conduct, and it is, therefore, difficult, if not impossible to envisage a situation which would truly be identifiable as an attempt rather than the completed crime itself. *Montgomery v McLeod* ((1977) SCCR Supp 164) provides something of a test. The police were called to the scene of a disturbance in a car park. The disturbance was being caused by a number of youths whom the police eventually succeeded in dispersing ... or at least they succeeded to the extent that all were persuaded to depart save one. The one who remained refused to go, and insisted on standing his ground. He declared that he was 'waiting for someone'. Since it was feared that the youths as a body might return and resume their disturbance if the police were not seen to be completely successful in emptying that car park, the obstinate youth was arrested. He was later convicted of breach of the peace — a decision that was affirmed on appeal. If attempted breach of the peace was truly a practical possibility, then surely the circumstances of this case afforded a realistic opportunity for its use; yet the Appeal Court appeared confident that the crime had been completed. The conclusion must be that the way in which breach of the peace is defined leaves no scope for attempt.

Corporations as accused

2.48   At one time, it was thought that legal (as opposed to human) *personae* could not commit common law crimes. The present position is that corporate bodies (see *Renton & Brown*, 13–23 to 13–26) can be convicted of some common law offences. They can, for example, be convicted of fraud (*Purcell Meats (Scotland) Ltd v McLeod* 1986 SCCR 672) provided that the actual human delinquents can be regarded as the controlling mind of the corporation concerned. Corporate bodies, however, cannot be convicted of offences which require *inter alia* the demonstration of some purely human characteristic, such as shamelessness (*Dean v John Menzies (Holdings) Ltd* 1981 JC 23). Against this background, it would appear that there was nothing to prevent a corporate person being convicted of a breach of the peace; but it is difficult to think of a situation where it would be realistic or worthwhile to proceed against the corporation rather than the human person(s) concerned. One assumes that a company might send threatening letters or orchestrate disturbances of the peace for some supposed business advantage. But there is something very odd in trying to envisage a company as having challenged someone to a fight, or as having shouted, cursed and sworn; and it may be that many types of breach-of-the-peace-conduct can only be indulged in by real human beings.

Multi-accused

2.49   It is a feature of breach of the peace that it often involves more than one person. In *Stirling v Herron* (1976 SLT (Notes) 2), for example, sixty-five persons were charged with breach of the peace by forming part of a disorderly crowd, bawling, shouting and swearing, and obstructing a footpath. Few Scottish court-houses are so designed that they might cope with such a large number of accused at any one time, and the device employed (where there are many pleas of not guilty) is to try the accused in batches of (say) six or seven at a time. Where that happens (as it did in *Stirling v Herron*) it has been held (again in *Stirling v Herron*) that there is in general no need for a different professional judge to deal with each trial, even though each trial concerns the self-same incident. It appears that a professional judge (such as a sheriff) can be trusted and expected to approach each such trial with an entirely open mind, and that no objection can, therefore, be made on the basis of bias or prejudice from that point of view. (*Quaere*, however, if a non-professional judge, such as a justice of a district court, can be trusted to dismiss findings in earlier trials from his mind.)

Circumstances and aggravations

General

2.50   'Breach of the peace is an offence the limits of which have never been sharply defined. It is so largely in each case a question of circumstances and of degree' (*Young v Heatly* 1959 JC 66 at 70, per Lord Justice-General Clyde). It is very common for judges and writers to stress the importance of circumstances *quoad* this particular offence (eg *Gordon*, 41–01; *Macdonald*, p 137; JSF, 'Breach of the Peace' 78 (1962) Sc Law Rev 73; *Raffaelli v Heatly* 1949 SLT 284 at 286, per Lord Mackay; *Ritchie v M'Phee* (1882) 5 Coup 147 at 149, per Lord Justice-Clerk Moncreiff — strictly on the requirements of the Glasgow Police Act 1866, s 135(5), but *a fortiori* breach of the peace). What is meant here was well encapsulated by Henry H Brown ('Breach of the Peace' (1895) 3 SLT (News) 151 and 163) when he argued that some conduct is *per se* by its very nature sufficient for breach of the peace, whereas other forms of behaviour might be innocuous *per se* unless circumstances to the contrary can be shown. Of the ten examples he quotes of the former class, the following three are certainly still valid in making his point — viz. challenging a person to a fight;

fighting, brawling and duelling; and, the uttering of verbal threats, if violent and pointed, to another. Such conduct would certainly be sufficient for breach of the peace, whatever the circumstances. On the other hand, Brown (citing *Marr v M'Arthur* (1878) 4 Coup 53) correctly points out that playing a sectarian air (Boyne Water) on a flute is not necessarily provocative to the point of breach of the peace unless the circumstances are special, as they would be if that tune were deliberately played in a staunchly Roman Catholic area or before an audience mainly composed of Roman Catholics. The same might be said generally of all alleged provocative behaviour. It can only be provocative in terms of the reasonable susceptabilities of the audience. Behaviour cannot be provocative in a vacuum. In a similar way, shouting and swearing could admit of an innocent explanation (as, for example, where one strikes one's thumb with a hammer-blow designed for a nail). And conduct indulged in in private is very much dependent on the circumstances if it is to be classed as breach of the peace (see **2.36** to **2.44**, above). There is, however, another role which circumstances can play *quoad* this offence. They can also act as aggravations of the crime (see **2.70** ff, below).

Circumstances — special susceptibility of audience

2.51 Conduct which is innocuous *per se* or *ex facie* neutral *quoad* breach of the peace may be elevated to criminal status by the special susceptibility of those who hear or see it. *Age and relationship*, for example, have been considered important from this point of view. In *Young v Heatly* (1959 JC 66) where the charges concerned indecent remarks made by a depute headmaster of a technical college, Lord Justice-General Clyde stressed (at p 70) that the remarks were directed at a series of adolescent boys (none older than 17 years) and made by a person to whom they could have expected to look for 'help and guidance'.

2.52 In some cases, an *atmosphere of tension and excitement (or volatility)* has been emphasised as having a significant bearing on whether what was done was sufficiently provocative. Thus, in *Saltman v Allan* (1988 SCCR 640), it would not have been entirely unexpected for a Scotsman to be shouting and swearing at 3.30 am on New Year's Day; but such behaviour became rather less trivial in the circumstances of the arrest of the accused's brother for a serious crime, and in the midst of a heavy police presence. Again, it might have been the case that a seven-second flaring of tempers on a football field during a match would have been ignored as a trivial foul, were it not for the fact that

that incident took place in full view of 43,000 spectators at a Rangers–Celtic game, where tensions and rivalries between the opposing fans were already evident and indeed only to be expected (*Butcher v Jessop* 1989 SCCR 119 at 130E, per Lord Justice-Clerk Ross).

Drunkenness

2.53 Drunkenness has also been considered as an important matter. What is meant here is the state of drunkenness of one's audience. As Lord Justice-Clerk Thomson once said (in *O'Hara v HMA* 1948 SLT 372 at 376): 'A man under the influence of alcohol as compared with a sober man may be readier to take offence, be more lacking in judgment, and be more prone to strike another.' Although this piece of judicial knowledge may be based more on folklore than on empirical research, it is a matter to be weighed in relation to any alleged provocative behaviour, and may explain Lord Murray's words in his dissenting speech in *Butcher v Jessop* (1989 SCCR 119 at 134C) — viz. 'The disorder of conduct has to be judged relative to the prevailing order. So conduct which is a breach of the peace in a public house may not be such in a public park'.

2.54 Even a sober audience may have sensibilities which the author of certain conduct ought to have had in mind. Thus, to attend a meeting called for the support of a certain objective with the intention of vigorously opposing that objective may result in a charge of breach of the peace. The circumstances do, however, have to be as special as they were in *Sleigh & Russell v Moxey* ((1850) J Shaw 369). There, a meeting was called of all those opposed to a parliamentary bill which would have legalised the marriage of a man with his deceased wife's sister. The court seems to have taken the view that the meeting was intended for those opposed to the bill and not for those of any other persuasion. Thus it was that the court upheld the conviction of a barrister and an ironmonger who attended for the sole purpose of speaking in favour of the bill and who disrupted the meeting by doing so. An important criterion was that in so doing they were entirely out of sympathy with their audience. Had they been in sympathy with the majority, then the outcome might have been different — as it was in *Armour v Macrae* ((1886) 1 White 58). In that case, the meeting was a political one, open to all. The intention was that the views of a prospective parliamentary candidate should be heard and that he should receive the views of his prospective constituents. That one member of the audience harangued the meeting at length and was critical of the candidate may have been not to the liking of the chairman and the candidate himself. But it was held highly relevant that the majority of the meeting supported the speaker from the floor; and thus it was that the High Court quashed his conviction for breach of the peace. It follows that the *subject matter and the views of the majority* of the audience are important circumstantial considerations in any charge of breach of the peace in relation to a *meeting*.

2.55 Being out of sympathy with one's audience is also important in a wider context, beyond formal meetings. Although generally society favours the free expression of ideas and political opinion, circumstances may dictate that such freedoms be exercised in another place and at another time. In *Duffield v Skeen* (1981 SCCR 66), the two accused took up position outside Celtic Park, Glasgow, where a football match was due to take place. In fact they stood outside that stadium near the entrance specified for Celtic supporters and shouted political slogans favouring an end to British rule in Northern Ireland and supportive of the IRA. Although this might normally have been tolerated, it was found as a matter of fact that the huge majority of Celtic supporters were or would have been disgusted by the accuseds' remarks, and that the accused, having failed to heed police warnings to desist, were rightly convicted of breach of the peace. A similar decision is recorded in *Alexander v Smith* (1984 SLT 176 (Note)) where the accused insisted on trying to sell National Front 'literature' (the National Front being an extreme right-wing, political organisation) to persons again entering a football ground, even though many of such persons exhibited intense annoyance at his behaviour. (Again, the accused refused to desist when called upon to do so by the police.)

2.56 Breach of the peace entails (*inter alia*) disturbance of the standing peace of the *locus*. This is obviously a relative matter. Disturbance worthy of note in a changing room after a rugby match will obviously be a quite different thing from disturbance in a church during a service. Indeed, in a church, a certain level of decorum and quietness is no more than to be expected (see *Dougall v Dykes* (1861) 4 Irv 101 at 104, per Lord Ardmillan). Against such a background, the seizing of a communion cup by one debarred from partaking in the particular ritual involved (*Hugh Fraser* (1839) 2 Swin 436 — although the accused there was convicted of a statutory offence rather than breach of the peace), or the removing oneself from the body of the kirk in a noisy and irreverent fashion whenever a particular minister ascends the pulpit (*Dougall v Dykes*) is likely to be attended with particular annoyance to those gathered *in facie ecclesiae* and thus likely to be a fit subject for breach of the peace. As much might be said for unseemly conduct at a funeral or within the precincts of a hospital or at any other place where a certain level of peace is to be expected (eg an examination hall), even though such behaviour might be unremarkable in some other context.

2.57 Preaching or holding a religious service or meeting in the streets or other public place is obviously not criminal (*Hutton v Main* (1891) 3 White 41 at 44, per Lord Justice-Clerk Macdonald). Neither is holding a properly authorised public parade (*Deakin v Milne* (1882) 5 Coup 174 at 183–4, per Lord Justice-Clerk Moncreiff). But circumstances can turn any of these lawful activities into occasions meriting charges of breach of the peace. If it is known (or to be reasonably anticipated) that, for example, opponents will do their best to disrupt such a meeting, service or parade (especially by the use of violence); or if it is known (or to be reasonably anticipated) that great annoyance or inconvenience will be caused to the lieges by holding the same in public; or if it is known (or to be reasonably anticipated) that a disorderly crowd will be thereby gathered, then breach of the peace is a legitimate charge against the organiser(s), particularly if he (or they) fail(s) to desist when warned of the consequences (see *Hutton v Main; Deakin v Milne*).

2.58 It may also be of importance that the 'audience' for one's behaviour consists (or is likely to consist) of women. This conclusion (admittedly somewhat insulting to women) is tentatively to be drawn from Lord Mackay's opinion in *Raffaelli v Heatly* (1949 SLT 284). There the accused, from a vantage point on the pavement outside a house, peered late at night through a gap in curtains covering the window of a living-room. One might wonder what was amiss with that, since the negligence of the person who drew the curtains must enter the equation. Lord Mackay was convinced, however, that the criminality lay in this — that it was 'to the annoyance of the modesty of women, if persevered in' (at 285–6), and carried 'the hope of seeing what female modesty will properly desire to be unobserved by the public' (at 286). It is not at all clear what would have been the case in Lord Mackay's estimation if St Leonard's Hill, Edinburgh (the *locus*) had been found to consist of male residents only; and thus it may be better to consider the behaviour as meriting conviction for some other reason — such as, for example, that the accused's conduct at that hour (11.50 pm) was highly alarming or annoying to at least some of those who witnessed it.

Circumstances — place

2.59   What would not excite particular attention in some contexts will certainly do so in others. Thus, making feline noises, lampooning the words of a song, or referring to persons as idiots will normally attract nothing more than curiosity; but the same cannot be said if these things are done in a place where a religious meeting is being held. It was, therefore, held to be a breach of the peace to behave in such fashions at a place where a meeting was being held by the Salvation Army (*Hendry v Ferguson* (1883) 5 Coup 278). Similarly, it would be a breach of the peace for such unseemly behaviour to occur in a church. As Lord Ardmillan said in *Dougall v Dykes* ((1861) 4 Irv 101 at 104): 'Decorum of conduct in a church is most important'. These cases and such a *dictum* give the impression that the place where the conduct occurs is important. But that is only partly true. The truly important criterion is that a religious service or meeting was there taking place and that it was attended by particular people who either were, or were likely to be annoyed or disturbed by such behaviour. The conduct in question (eg marching noisily from a church, seizing hold of a communion cup — see **2.56**, above) would have been quite immaterial if the church or hall had been deserted at the time. Exactly the same criterion (*mutatis mutandis*) pertains in respect of public houses, sports stadia (see *Butcher v Jessop* 1989 SCCR 119), buses (see *McLean v McNaughton* 1984 SCCR 319) and other candidates for 'place' as a circumstance determining whether particular conduct can be sufficient for breach of the peace. It is not so much the place that matters, but rather what is taking place and who is, or is likely to be there at the time. (Where the place is a private one, special considerations may, however, apply: see **2.36** to **2.44**, above.)

Circumstances — previous complaints

2.60   Where there is some doubt as to whether particular conduct is sufficient for breach of the peace, previous complaints of annoyance or alarm in respect of similar behaviour in the immediate past have been considered material. In some cases, such complaints would tend to show that the accused was fully aware of the likely results of his conduct — as in *Deakin v Milne* ((1882) 5 Coup 174 at 185, per Lord Craighill) where the organiser of a Salvation Army procession ought to have known from previous parades what the consequences might be — ie at the very least complaints (but also probably actual disturbances) on the part of those opposed to the Army's philosophy and practices. Taking account of such circumstances, or indeed treating past history as circumstances at all, seems extremely tenuous, however, where the accused was not necessarily the person previously involved and might not know that there had been any previous incidents. Nevertheless, in *Raffaelli v Heatly* (1949 SLT 284), both Lord Justice-Clerk Thomson and Lord Mackay considered it significant that previous 'peeping-tom' incidents had occurred in the same street, and that Mrs Price (an eye-witness) had been so alarmed by them as to inform the police. What should have mattered, one imagines, is whether Mrs Price had been alarmed by the accused's actings on the night in question, and not whether she had been alarmed on some previous occasion. (This is especially so since the accused was found not guilty of having acted as he did on any prior occasion in that part of Edinburgh.) Such circumstances, however, are regularly taken account of. (See, for example, *Stewart v Jessop* (1988 SCCR 492) where the fact that there had been previous complaints from residents about youths drinking in a certain close and causing annoyance there was considered material to the conviction of five young men for breach of the peace. They had been discovered by the police in the self-same close, drinking lager at 11.30 pm. There seemed little need to rely on prior complaints at all, however. The youths were causing a minor disturbance late at night, had refused to move on when requested to do so, and also had visited the police with verbal abuse (which, even making all due allowances for limited vocabulary, had clearly been intended to annoy).)

Circumstances — repetition of conduct

2.61 Particularly in relation to the more minor forms of conduct relevant to breach of the peace, it has often been held to be a material circumstance that the conduct was repeated, or was not desisted from after a request to do so from (say) the police. There may be two principal reasons for this. First, repetition within a short space of time means that a series of minor acts may be added together to amount to something worth prosecuting. Secondly, repetition may indicate a plan or design in relation to the conduct in question. Although intent to annoy or disturb is not necessary for conviction (see **2.31**, above), the possibility that such intent exists again reinforces the view that the total conduct is worthy of prosecution.

2.62 Examples of cases where repetition of the conduct in question has been taken into account are legion. Thus, in *Hugh Fraser* ((1839) 2 Swin 436) the accused was debarred from taking communion by his church in 1835, but insisted on attempting to do so in 1836, 1837 and 1838. Although he was ultimately convicted of an alternative statutory offence ('troubling the kirk', con. the Act 11th Parl Jac VI c 27, 1587 — see APS III, p 430, c 6) rather than breach of the peace, the indictment for *inter alia* breach of the peace specifically narrated the repetition of the conduct and the refusal of the accused to desist when requested to do so by the minister and other members of the congregation. Also, in *Dougall v Dykes* ((1861) 4 Irv 101) the accused had noisily risen from his seat and left the parish church of East Kilbride whenever the Reverend William Carrick entered the pulpit to begin divine service. This, however, was done not just once, but on a number of Sundays between August 1860 and March 1861. Lord Neaves, in particular, drew attention to the oft repeated nature of the conduct and continued (at 105): '... the acts set forth are such as might very naturally admit of the construction, that they were intended as an insult to the minister; and I cannot doubt that a series of such insults, repeated Sunday after Sunday, or time after time, may amount to a breach of the peace.' Similarly, in *Hendry v Ferguson* ((1883) 5 Coup 278) the accused was convicted of breach of the peace in that he attended a Salvation Army meeting and did his best to disrupt it by (*inter alia*) screaming at the top of his voice, lustily singing secular words in place of the proper lines of hymns, making noises like a cat, and calling speakers 'idiots' when they were attempting to address the meeting. It was a material point that he consistently refused to desist from these tactics or to leave the hall (until at long last a police constable was summoned).

2.63   In a more secular vein, it was held to be an important consideration by Lord Justice-Clerk Thomson (at 285) and Lord Mackay (at 286) that the accused in *Raffaelli v Heatly* (1949 SLT 284) peered through a gap in the curtains of a living room at No 10 St Leonard's Hill, Edinburgh, not once but twice. (After peering though the window for about two to three minutes, he had walked off down the street for approximately ten yards before turning and resuming his attentions to the same window.) Lord Justice-General Clyde also made particular mention of repetition in *Young v Heatly* (1959 JC 66 at 70) where he drew attention to 'the fact that they [the interviews where indecent remarks were made] took place within a matter of hours with a series of adolescent boys...'. (It must be noted, however, that it would have been necessary from the point of view of proof for there to have been a connected series of such acts, since the only witness to each was the boy being interviewed — see *Moorov v HM Advocate* 1930 JC 68; *Tudhope v Hazelton* 1984 SCCR 455.)

2.64   Shouting and swearing in particular is a form of breach of the peace where refusal to desist may be material to the offence. (But cf *McMillan v Normand* 1989 SCCR 269.) This follows from *Logan v Jessop* (1987 SCCR 604), as the decision in that case has subsequently been interpreted. The facts were simple. The police received word of a possible disturbance at Westray Circus, Glasgow, and, indeed, when they arrived at the *locus*, ten to twelve youths were seen loitering and heard shouting obscenities. When the youths spied the police, they made off. The police, however, waited in anticipation that some of the youths might return, and were duly rewarded by the return of the two accused. They shouted at the police 'Fuck off' and 'You cunts are always digging us up'. For this, and this alone, they were arrested, and were subsequently convicted for breach of the peace by a district court. On appeal, their convictions were quashed. Although the decision seemed to turn on the basis that no members of the public (other than police) had in fact been proved to be within ear-shot to be annoyed at the time these utterances were made, such a ground of decision would have been contrary to what was thought to be settled law (see **2.16**, above) and was rapidly discredited (eg in *Stewart v Jessop* 1988 SCCR 492; and, *Norris v McLeod* 1988 SCCR 572). The true basis of the decision is thought to be that given by Sheriff Hamilton in *Norris v McLeod*, viz. — that the accused in *Logan* were simply expressing forthright opinions to the police in the only language available to them, their vocabulary range being severely limited. If they had repeatedly used such language to the police in question, especially if warned about it and called upon to desist, then the decision of the Appeal Court might have been different. In *Norris v McLeod* itself, for example, the accused was incensed that the police had suspected him of theft and that they had insisted (fruitlessly, as it turned out) on searching a bag he had been carrying. He shouted and swore at them, and continued to do so despite two warnings to behave himself. The Appeal Court there had no doubt that the prolonged abuse fully justified the conviction, and that the case of *Logan v Jessop* was to be distinguished. (The decision in *Stewart v Jessop* can probably also be explained on the same basis, viz. that the swearing and abuse there was sustained after the delivery by the police of a warning to the accused youths that they should behave themselves.)

2.65   As a final (and striking) example, the accused in *Montgomery v McLeod* ((1977) SCCR Supp 164) was convicted of breach of the peace in that he obstinately refused to obey an instruction from the police to remove himself from a car park where, a few minutes earlier, a disturbance had taken place. Police had succeeded with some difficulty in ridding the *locus* of the youths responsible for the fracas, and were afraid that if even one person was seen to remain (ie the accused), then the youths might regroup and occasion further mischief. The accused, however, refused all pleas that he should depart — ie that he should desist from his 'conduct' which was deemed likely to cause disturbance if it were allowed to continue. His conviction for breach of the peace was, therefore, upheld by the Appeal Court because of his refusal to refrain from what he was 'doing'.

Circumstances and alarm or annoyance

2.66 Actual alarm or annoyance (or indeed any other recognised mental state) need not be proved on the part of any particular person for there to be a conviction for breach of the peace (*Young v Heatly* 1959 JC 66 at 70, per Lord Justice-General Clyde). (That conclusion may not have followed so easily from the earlier cases of *Ferguson v Carnochan* ((1889) 2 White 278) and *Raffaelli v Heatly* (1949 SLT 284) as the Lord Justice-General seems to have thought. He can, for example, be seen (at 70) to be quoting from Lord Justice-Clerk Thomson's account of counsel's arguments in *Raffaelli v Heatly* (at 285) rather than from what was actually decided there by the court. But a decision of the High Court is binding on all lower courts (*Jessop v Stevenson* 1988 SLT 223 at 225) whatever its pedigree, and Lord Justice-General Clyde's conclusion is now widely accepted). What really matters is that the conduct of the accused occurred or took effect in a place where other people could reasonably have been expected to be present — ie other people who might reasonably have been alarmed or annoyed (or whatever) by it (see **2.49**, above). This involves the drawing of an inference; and whether it can be drawn will depend on all the circumstances of an individual case. In *Young v Heatly* itself, for example, the circumstances were listed as including (since Lord Justice-General Clyde mysteriously alluded to other 'special' ones at p 70) the 'disgusting nature of the suggestions made, the fact that they took place within a matter of hours with a series of adolescent boys, and the fact that they were made to pupils by a depute headmaster to whom they would normally have looked for help and guidance' (p 70). Thus, the nature of the conduct itself, its repetition within a short period of time, the age of those addressed, and their relationship to the accused at the time of the conduct were considered as together permitting the necessary inference to be drawn that breach of the peace had been committed. (Whether the inference in *Young* could reasonably have been drawn *stante* these circumstances is open to doubt — see **2.42**, above.) It would seem, therefore, that only a combination of circumstances would suffice where no actual alarm or annoyance (or whatever) could be demonstrated.

2.67 Even where actual alarm or annoyance (or whatever) can be shown, it is thought that that would not automatically justify a conviction for breach of the peace. The general definitions of the crime (see **2.15** to **2.22**, above) all emphasise the importance of reasonableness; and it is thought proper and just for an assertion of (say) alarm to be tested accordingly. 'Was it reasonable for the witness to be alarmed or annoyed (or whatever) as a result of the accused's behaviour?' should always be asked — as it was, for example, by the sheriff in *Taylor v Hamilton* (1984 SCCR 393 — a case concerned with whether alarm said to have been caused by the sight of glue-sniffing might suffice for breach of the peace). But the answer will again depend on all the circumstances of any particular case.

Circumstances — time

2.68 There are two ways in which time can be important. First, since breach of the peace involves breaking or the likelihood of breaking the 'standing peace' of the place where conduct occurs or takes effect, 'real time' (ie the time of day) will obviously have some bearing on what that 'standing peace' is. The 'standing peace' of the streets in a town is one thing when a carnival is passing through them, and quite another at 2 am on a Sunday morning. It was, therefore, highly material to the conviction in *Ferguson v Carnochan* ((1889) 2 White 278) that the swearing and noise could be heard in the public streets at between 3 am and 4 am of a Sunday morning — a time when a reasonable level of quietness was to be expected. Similarly, time was considered to be relevant in *Raffaelli v Heatly* (1949 SLT 284) where Lord Mackay opined that the conduct significantly took place at 11.30 pm (11.50 pm was quoted in the complaint, although the discrepancy is immaterial), on a September evening when not only would the streets be quiet but also 'when it may be many women are making for bed or already in bed' (at 286). Obviously 'peeping tom' activities at such an hour would be 'calculated' (ie likely) to cause considerable alarm, and indeed would be more likely to achieve their object. Again, in a similar vein, discharging a firearm in the streets of a town is likely to prove alarming at any time, but even more so at 2 am. As Lord Justice-General Emslie put it (in *Palazzo v Copeland* 1976 JC 52 at 53): '[T]he act of firing a gun in the air in an urban situation at that time in the morning [2 am] was calculated to be likely [sic] to put lieges in general in a state of fear and alarm.' 'Real time' can also lead to a reasonable inference that other people would have been likely to be in the vicinity of the conduct. Thus in *Boyle v Wilson* (1988 SCCR 485), Lord Justice-General Emslie (at 487) took the view that shouting, singing and swearing in the middle of Greenock at 3.10 pm on a Sunday afternoon in May would certainly have occurred where other people were likely to be.

2.69 Secondly, time is important from the point of view of the duration of the conduct in question. The longer it continues, the more likely that reasonable persons may be alarmed, annoyed (or whatever) by it. (Thus, in *Thompson v MacPhail* (1989 SCCR 266) Lord Brand (at 268D) felt it might have been material how long the accused had remained in a locked toilet cubicle, since the longer the duration, the more likely that he would have been discovered in the sanguineous act of injecting himself.) Equally, the longer it is indulged in, the less likely it will be that that conduct has an innocent explanation. Once again this is illustrated by *Raffaelli v Heatly* (1949 SLT 284), where Lord Mackay took the view (at 286) that standing for two to three minutes at a time to peer through a gap in curtains into a lighted room was inconsistent with innocence. The duration of the conduct could not be squared with a mere glancing-in out of curiosity 'en passant'.

Aggravations

2.70

'Further, the detention was in itself of a most oppressive kind. The man was charged with a paltry offence — breach of the peace — and he was to be kept in prison for a time [seven days] which would have been a severe punishment for such an offence, unless it was aggravated.'

This *obiter* remark of Lord Justice-Clerk Macdonald (*Kelly v Rowan* (1897) 2 Adam 357 at 361) shows that breach of the peace offences may be aggravated, and that generally a significant prison sentence would be unusual for such a crime unless it was aggravated.

2.71 In the nineteenth century, criminal charges were verbose and invariably specified aggravations as part of the major premiss. These could easily be identified in the 'major' by the initial words 'especially when' or 'more especially when' which preceded their narration. It is not now the practice to point-up, or even mention at all, such aggravations as the prosecutor thinks appropriate for the consideration of the court; but it is still possible to conclude that certain matters do amount to *de facto* aggravations. Thus, if it is accepted that no particular form of *mens rea* is required for conviction of breach of the peace (see **2.31**, above) then the actual existence of *mens rea* can be seen as an aggravation, as it was apparently alleged to be in *Dougall v*

Dykes ((1861) 4 Irv 101) where the indictment narrated that breach of the peace was especially heinous when it was committed 'wilfully and maliciously'. That case also indicates that the occasion of the behaviour and the susceptability of one's audience to the behaviour may be matters rendering the crime more serious. The particular points made by the indictment in *Dougall v Dykes* were that the conduct (repeated and noisy egress from a church whenever the minister entered to begin the ritual) took place on the Sabbath, in presence of the minister and congregation (surely a better way to express the aggravation than the simplistic 'in church' specified in *Hugh Fraser* (1839) 2 Swin 436), and during divine service. Similar issues can also be seen in more modern cases. In *Butcher v Jessop* (1989 SCCR 119), for example, where players who had acted violently on the field of play were charged with breach of the peace, Sheriff McKay (in a passage uncontradicted by the Appeal Court except in relation to the use of the word 'assault') said (at 123F):

'If anything, a further breach of the peace [ie by the accused players against the background of breaches of the peace committed by members of the crowd attending the match] in the form of conduct, albeit by way of assault, which might reasonably be expected to cause the fans to be upset and annoyed and to take reprisals at their own hand is aggravated when set against this highly combustible background' [ie a crowd of 43,000 persons, composed of volatile Rangers and Celtic supporters].

Similarly, it might not be thought *ex facie* that shouting and swearing was a particularly serious offence, but the 19-year-old accused in *McGivern v Jessop* (1988 SCCR 511) was sentenced to three months' detention for just that. The important matter there was again the occasion of the swearing. The accused (in company with other 'soccer casuals' — smartly dressed youths whose object was 'to make trouble for fun' [per Lord Brand at 513]) was taunting Celtic Football-Club supporters as they passed along the streets of Glasgow with shouts of 'Fucking wanks', 'Fuck off wankers', 'Fenian bastards' and similar coarse expressions. The recipients of this torrent of abuse were plainly upset (and by reputation likely to respond aggressively), and the Appeal Court clearly felt that condign punishment was fully justified.

2.72   Prior convictions are obviously aggravating circumstances; but unlike nineteenth and early twentieth century criminal charges, it is not now permissible to narrate that the accused has these in the body of the complaint (Criminal Procedure (Scotland) Act 1975, s 356(1)). However, they may be taken account of after conviction when the court is considering sentence (1975 Act, s 356(2)), and this is (of course) of regular occurrence. In *Tait v Allan* (1984 SCCR 385), for example, the accused was sentenced to sixty days in prison for breach of the peace, mainly on account of his long criminal record. Significant terms of imprisonment for such an offence usually indicate the presence of one or more aggravating factors; and thus the decision to imprison the accused in *Young v Heatly* (1959 JC 66) for thirty days requires some explanation. It is difficult, however, to disentangle the circumstances which were thought necessary to justify conviction there from the circumstances which were thought to be aggravations. It does not seem to be the case that the accused in *Young* had any significant criminal record; but it was true that the addressees of his indecent remarks were pupils (or students) of his and who would normally have looked to him 'for help and guidance' (Lord Justice-General Clyde at 70). From this, it may follow that the age of, and relationship one has to, one's 'victim' are aggravating circumstances.

2.73 The status of 'victim' or accused may also be of importance. Although this has never been made the subject of express decision, in the case of *HM Advocate v Hayes* (1973 SLT 202) the indictment (since this instance of sending threatening letters was 'a very serious crime' (per Lord Cameron at 203) — see **2.11**, above) stressed that the sending of explosives together with a threatening letter was done 'with intent to menace William Armstrong, a senior officer in the prison service at Her Majesty's Prison at Porterfield, Inverness, in the discharge of his duties at said Prison'. It is thought that these words disclose an aggravation in that the conduct was made much worse by the status of its intended victim. Similarly, in *Dyce v Aitchison* (1985 SCCR 184), the complaint specifically mentioned that the accused's conduct in the dock included threats of violence made 'towards Sheriff Booker-Milburn who was then on the bench' — echoing perhaps the age-old aggravation that conduct had taken place 'whilst the judge(s) were sitting in judgment' (see, for example, the Act 1593 c 22 — APS IV p 22). It is not entirely clear whether shouting and swearing at, for example, a police officer is any worse than behaving in such fashion towards a civilian; but following the same line as is suggested can be traced from the foregoing authorities, in *Worsfold v Walkingshaw* (1987 SCCR 17) Sheriff Smith imposed a significant fine of £100 on a person who had so behaved, giving as one of his reasons for doing so (at 18) that he 'regarded it as an aggravation that a police cadet as well as a police officer had been subjected to this discourtesy'. (This particular part of the learned sheriff's decision was not objected to on appeal.)

2.74 As far as the status of the accused himself is concerned, it is usually regarded as an aggravation that a breach of the peace was committed by a 'peace officer'. Thus, in the early case of *Thomas Whitfield* ((1843) 1 Broun 609) where the charges involved mobbing, breach of the peace and assault, the court considered (as reported at p 611) 'that a riot committed by soldiers, whose duty it was to preserve the peace, was a most serious offence . . .'. *A fortiori*, any breach of the peace (as indeed any other offence) committed by a police officer will probably be regarded as aggravated by his status (though cf *Carey v Tudhope* 1984 SCCR 157, where only 120 hours of community service were imposed on a police officer who *inter alia* had behaved thoroughly aggressively towards his 'victim', put him into a state of fear and shouted at him: 'If you turn round I'll put your face through that grille, or if I don't I'll kick your arse through it. And if I'm in the van I'll run you over.'

2.75 It is thought that a 'bad' motive may well be an aggravating factor in relation to breach of the peace and probably crimes in general. Thus, to taunt football supporters with well-chosen obscene expressions *for fun* may be taken as involving a 'bad' motive (see *McGivern v Jessop* 1988 SCCR 511). Conversely, 'good' motives may not be relevant *quoad* conviction (*Palazzo v Copeland* 1976 JC 52), but should be taken account of at sentence by way of mitigation. Some decisions, however, appear to deny that motive has any relevance at all. In *Donaghy v Tudhope* (1985 SCCR 118), for example, in an appeal against sentence as oppressive on *(inter alia)* the ground that the accused had been motivated by social conscience, Lord Justice-General Emslie in delivering the opinion of the court said this (at 120):

'We are not concerned with the motive which led to the commission of this offence [breach of the peace]. We have already mentioned that it was a grave one of its kind and we have no reason to think for one minute that the sentence imposed [60 days in prison] upon this appellant was any more severe than the sentence which would have been imposed upon somebody who did not enjoy his social conscience.'

It is not thought that this decision leads to any general view that motive is irrelevant to sentence. The courts in Scotland are, and must be seen to be apolitical. Here, the accused's motive was a political one — as was evidenced by the slogans on the banners he and his fellows hung from the jibs of the tower-cranes they had climbed, viz. 'Glasgow's Miles Better without Trident' and 'Turn the Tide on War'. The accused was further resident in a 'Peace Camp', and his purpose in climbing and occupying a tower-crane was the disruption of building work on a site where the Ministry of Defence headquarters were being erected. All of this had a distinct political flavour, being designed to subvert government policy and the will of Parliament. It is not, therefore, surprising at all that in this case, the court could give no credence to motive.

2.76   As breach of the peace is essentially a minor offence (see **2.08** to **2.12**, above), it may be that a genuine declaration of remorse in respect of one's conduct could be to one's advantage at sentence, and, conversely, that a complete failure to recognise one's fault may tend to aggravation. As much was arguably held in *McLean v McNaughton* (1984 SCCR 319). There, a 16-year-old schoolboy had lit a firework and tossed it down the centre aisle of a bus in which he and several others were travelling. The result was considerable alarm verging on panic if not hysteria. Some passengers tried to extinguish the fuse; others attempted to alight from the vehicle whilst it was yet in motion; and, when the firework eventually exploded, one elderly man was so startled that be began shouting 'bombs!', thereby adding to the general alarm and confusion. The accused youth did not at once confess that he was the culprit, although he did eventually plead guilty. Regrettably, however, he persisted in showing no remorse at all for his actions, with the result that the reports submitted anent him by a social worker and an assistant governor of a remand institution were unfavourable, simply underlining for the court his irresponsibility and complete lack of concern. (He was sentenced to three months' detention.)

2.77   It is not permissible to treat some issues as aggravations of breach of the peace (though once again this is probably a matter of general application in the Scottish criminal justice system). It is not, for example, proper to treat a particular breach of the peace as aggravated by virtue of its also being a breach of an interdict (*Friend v Normand* 1988 SCCR 232), although it is difficult to see why not. If the accused is aware that he is prohibited from molesting (say) his wife or from entering the matrimonial home without her express permission, surely the fact that in deliberate breach thereof he had gone to her home, shouted and sworn, demanded admission and eventually broken down the door should have rendered the situation a much worse breach of the peace than one executed where there was no such interdict. Slightly easier to accept is the rule that a court cannot find breach of the peace aggravated by reference to other charges to which the accused has pled not guilty — such pleas having been accepted by the prosecutor. However much the court may be tempted to conclude that the accused was probably guilty of these too, and that the prosecutor had been unwise to accept the pleas, such temptation must be resisted (*Worsfold v Walkingshaw* 1987 SCCR 17).

2.78   There is one statutory aggravation over which in relation to breach of the peace there is some doubt. According to s 290 of the Criminal Procedure (Scotland) Act 1975:

'Where a person is convicted by the sheriff of . . . (b) a second or subsequent offence inferring personal violence, he may, without prejudice to any wider powers conferred by statute, be sentenced to imprisonment for any period not exceeding six months.'

In the case of *Adair v Morton* (1972 SLT (Notes) 70) the accused was charged with malicious mischief, as also with breach of the peace in that he did 'conduct himself in a disorderly manner, bawl and shout, curse and swear'. He admitted the charge and also agreed that his breach of the peace had included threats of (personal?) violence (cf the 'facts' as stated in (1973) 37 JCL 68). He also admitted a prior conviction for assault. The sheriff took the view that the current offence of breach of the peace was on the 'facts' (these having been narrated by the prosecutor) one inferring personal violence, and he imposed a prison sentence of six months. On appeal, that sentence was cut to three months. Unfortunately, the Appeal Court delivered no opinions in respect of this case, but is reported to have decided that as 'personal violence was not involved in the charge as *libelled*' (1972 SLT (Notes) at 70), the statutory aggravation did not apply. Given that there can be a close connection between breach of the peace and assault (see *Johnstone v Lindsay* (1906) 5 Adam 192 at 195, per Lord Justice-Clerk Macdonald; and *Butcher v Jessop* 1989 SCCR 119 at 131D–E, per Lord Justice-Clerk Ross and at 134G–135A, per Lord Murray (dissenting)), it is uncertain what the value of this decision is. It could be that it is authority for the proposition that breach of the peace can never be an offence inferring personal violence, a proposition for which there is some support (see, for example, *Wishart v Heatly* 1949 SLT 129; *Russo v Robertson* 1951 SLT 408 — both, however, decisions on the interpretation of now repealed legislation). But it would be difficult to reconcile that proposition with even the standard statutory styles for charges of breach of the peace (see **2.02**, above). Again, the decision could simply be authority for the proposition that a breach of the peace charge must expressly libel 'personal violence' matters in some way, in order for that charge to be received as one inferring personal violence. It is difficult to reconcile this too, however, with some of the later decisions, particularly that of *Butcher v Jessop*, where Lord Justice-Clerk Ross (Lord Allanbridge concurring) said this (at 129B): 'There are many forms of conduct which are capable of constituting disorderly conduct, and whenever a charge is framed in this form [viz. 'You did conduct yourself in a disorderly manner and commit a breach of the peace'], evidence of disorderly conduct will require to be led. Acts of violence are just one type of conduct which may constitute disorderly conduct, and as to which the prosecutor will require to lead evidence.' The acts of violence to which the Lord Justice-Clerk referred were clearly acts of *personal* violence in *Butcher*. It may simply be that in *Adair v Morton*, despite the way in which the report is worded in the SLT and JCL, what the court meant was that the facts disclosed drunken, loutish behaviour and wanton damage — but nothing approaching *personal* violence. There seems no reason in principle why a conviction for breach of the peace (even of the uninformative 'disorderly conduct' type) should not (depending on the facts) be received as one inferring personal violence; but bearing in mind that breach of the peace is essentially a minor offence attracting minor penalties, in such a case should not the charge have properly been (or included) one of assault?

Defences

General

2.79 In an early article on 'Breach of the Peace' ((1895) 3 SLT (News) 151 and 163, at 165), Henry H Brown (presumably the co-author of *Renton & Brown* and sometime fiscal of Forfarshire and Midlothian) considered the defences which were most often tendered in response to breach of the peace charges. His first suggestion of 'not guilty' seems very strange. At best it amounts to the 'defence' that the prosecutor is put to the trouble of proving his case. But the modern view involves coupling the plea of 'not guilty' to something more positive by way of defence, such as an assertion of alibi or incrimination (see *Macdonald*, p 265 on these rather obvious issues). Brown's second and third suggestions were arguably untenable in his own day, and are certainly so now, viz. that no-one was annoyed or disturbed, and that the public peace was not broken (on which, see **2.15** to **2.23**, above). In the modern law, it would be quite insufficient to argue that no-one was disturbed or annoyed (or whatever) in fact unless one could also demonstrate that no *reasonable* person could have been so affected by the conduct, assuming that the conduct occurred, or took effect in a place, or in circumstances where such a person might *reasonably* have been found (which *per se* introduces a separate, possible line of defence). The same holds for the assertion that the public peace was not broken. The real issue concerns whether it might reasonably have been broken, given all the relevant circumstances, and therein lies the possible angle of defence.

2.80 Brown's final two suggestions for defences cover self-defence (on which see **2.97**, below) and legitimate excuse. As with his other 'common' defences, no examples are provided whatsoever. That there was or was not a legitimate excuse sounds more in keeping with prosecutorial discretion as to whether to proceed on a police report (a matter expressly referred to in all editions of *Renton & Brown*, from the first edition in 1909 (p 6) to the current (5th) at 3-01). But such a 'defence' might have lain behind the curious quashing of the conviction in *Shannon v Skeen* ((1977) SCCR Supp 180). There two (male) private detectives were hired by the prospective purchaser of a vending machine company. Their task was to find out such vital commercial information as how often the machines were attended to, and this they achieved by following in their motor car a female employee whose job was to empty the machines of their cash content. The employee rapidly became aware of their attentions to her activities, and rapidly (and understandably) became alarmed. After a total of one and half hours of their persistent following, she was reduced to a state of abject distress and called the police. They seemed satisfied with the two men's explanation, but still tendered a report to the fiscal. The result was a prosecution for breach of the peace. The salient part of the charge in the complaint read that they did conduct themselves 'in a disorderly manner, persistently follow in motor car registration number . . . [the female employee] . . . and commit a breach of the peace'. There was no suggestion that this was not a perfectly relevant charge (see *Mackie v MacLeod* (March 1961, unreported) High Court; (*Gordon* 41-06) for its double), but the conviction recorded in the sheriff court was quashed on appeal, the High Court simply holding that the facts found did not contain sufficient material to justify such a verdict. Perhaps a stronger explanation (though not necessarily a just one in the circumstances) would have been that the accused, in the opinion of the appeal court, had sufficient excuse for their conduct. In a similar way, in *Norris v McLeod* (1988 SCCR 572) where the accused fell under police suspicion of dishonesty, and had his bag searched in consequence, he would have had some excuse for giving vent immediately to his feelings when the police suspicions were proved groundless; but such excuse as he had was rapidly dissipated by the prolonged and persistent abuse which he then heaped on the unfortunate policemen's heads.

Accident

2.81   Although little discussed in textbooks, there is no doubt that Scots law recognises a defence of accident and that such a defence cannot be confined to alleged homicide by stabbing (as was the factual situation in the 'accident' case of *Mackenzie v HM Advocate* 1983 SLT 220). In particular, there is no reason to suppose that it might not be pled in answer to a charge of breach of the peace in an appropriate case. Such a case might arise if an innocent bystander were to be swept into the midst of a crowd which was conducting itself in a disorderly fashion, shouting and swearing at the police and throwing missiles (see **2.45** to **2.46**, above). If such a person were to be seized during a police foray into that crowd, it would not be necessary to show that he himself shouted, swore or threw anything in order for a conviction of breach of the peace to be returned (*Tudhope v O'Neill* 1983 SCCR 443). He also might be well aware of the 'plan' which the crowd was executing (see *MacNeill v Robertson* 1982 SCCR 468; *Tudhope v Morrison* 1983 SCCR 262); but it is thought that a defence of *accidental* presence in that crowd might have some reasonable chance of success. All he need do, after all, is cast doubt on the Crown's ability to show the contrary.

Coercion

2.82   In some cases of breach of the peace, particularly the forms which relate to participation with a mob or crowd in disorderly acts, coercion appears to be a competent and credible defence. It is not at all unlikely that a group of 'evilly disposed' persons may seek to augment their numbers and skills by pressing innocent bystanders into their ranks. That might be achieved by physical compulsion (which is probably a distinguishable defence) or by fear induced by threats. If it were achieved by the latter, then the innocent recruits might have a defence based on the overpowering compulsion of those threats coupled to their own inabilities, in the circumstances, to resist or obtain help. *Hume's* examples of cases involving the defence of 'compulsion' or 'constraint by force' all involve situations of that nature:

'A mob, for instance, or tumultuous convocation, are moving on their enterprise; and on their way, as sometimes happens, they take possession of such as they meet, and compel them, in appearance at least, to take a part in the adventure, and augment their strength. Certainly such an allegation, duly qualified, and made out by apt *indicia*, and not contradicted by other circumstances in the man's behaviour, is relevant to acquit him of the charge' (*Hume* I, pp 51–52; other, non-hypothetical cases of a similar nature from the seventeenth and early eighteenth centuries are set out between pp 51 and 53).

Although most of the examples found in *Hume* were taken by him from less well 'regulated' (meaning 'policed') times, it is not necessary for there to be a situation verging on anarchy before the defence can be realised. Nor is it necessary that there should be a mob or crowd (see *Thomson v HM Advocate* 1983 SCCR 368). It is thought also that *Hume's* qualifications (p 53) that there should be 'an immediate danger of death or great bodily harm; [and] an inability to resist the violence' relate only to an 'atrocious crime'. They have certainly been endorsed as essential for the defence in a case of armed robbery on a post office (*Thomson v HM Advocate*). Presumably, these qualifications would also be essential in relation to a serious case of mobbing and rioting. But, in *Thomson v HM Advocate* (at 381), it is stated that '[a] defence of coercion is recognised in the law of Scotland . . . [and] Hume restricts it to "atrocious crimes".' This, however, is an *obiter dictum* and must amount to a misreading of the passage in question. *Hume* simply writes (at p 53) that the defence 'is at least somewhat a difficult plea, and can hardly be serviceable in the case of a trial for any atrocious crime, unless it have the support of [the two qualifications quoted above] . . .'. Perhaps, then, threats of sufficient immediacy but well short of death or serious bodily injury may suffice for coercion in relation to ordinary breaches of the peace which are not by nature 'atrocious crimes'. (It should be noted that Hume's remaining two qualifications for 'atrocious crimes' — viz. 'a backward and an inferior part in the perpetration; and a disclosure of the fact, as well as restitution of the spoil, on the first safe and convenient occasion' — were treated in *Thomson v HM Advocate* (at 380) as being non-essential. They were simply matters which might be used to reinforce or discredit the genuineness of the accused's story that he had been coerced.)

Diminished responsibility

2.83 'Any mental or pathological condition short of insanity — any question of diminished responsibility owing to any cause, which does not involve insanity — is relevant only to the question of mitigating circumstances and sentence' (*HM Advocate v Cunningham* 1963 JC 80 at 84, per Lord Justice-General Clyde). This well-known quotation provides authority that diminished responsibility (as opposed to insanity — see **2.86**, below) cannot constitute a full defence, but may act in mitigation of sentence. There is no reason, therefore, why this should not apply *de facto* in cases of breach of the peace, given that the 'definition' of diminished responsibility is wide (viz: 'that there must be aberration or weakness of mind; that there must be some form of mental unsoundness; that there must be a state of mind which is bordering on, though not amounting to, insanity; that there must be a mind so affected that responsibility is diminished from full responsibility to partial responsibility . . .', per Lord Justice-Clerk Alness in *HM Advocate v Savage* 1923 JC 49 at 51 — cited with approval by a full bench in *Brennan v HM Advocate* 1977 SLT 151 at 154). The reason for adding the phrase *de facto* to the applicability of 'diminished responsibility' to breach of the peace lies in this — that in *HM Advocate v Cunningham* (Lord Justice-General Clyde at 84) and again in *Brennan v HM Advocate* (opinion of the court at 155) it was expressly stated that this 'defence' was applicable only to a charge of murder and not to a lesser one. Such statements must have been intended to emphasise that the reduction of a charge from a serious one to a lesser one is not to be operated outside murder. Indeed, there is obviously no way in which effect can be given to the mitigatory properties of diminished responsibility where such a charge has been preferred other than by reducing it to culpable homicide (given that murder carries a fixed sentence of life in prison — Criminal Procedure (Scotland) Act 1975, s 205). In any event, sentence is a matter for the discretion of the judge; and if a person has been convicted before him of breach of the peace, what may be taken into account in the exercise of that discretion is at large. As a matter of practice, issues involving diminished responsibility certainly seem to be taken into consideration in crimes well below the status of murder. In *Carmichael v Boyle* (1985 SLT 399), for example, where the accused's mental abilities had certainly been diminished by hypoglycaemia, Sheriff Boyle, when ordered by the Appeal Court to convict of assault, breach of the peace, and contraventions of s 41(1)(a) of the Police (Scotland) Act 1967, imposed by way of sentence an admonition only (see 1985 SCCR 71, Sheriff Gordon's commentary at point 6). This is a not unimportant consideration since many of the more bizarre forms of breach of the peace may indicate that their authors are mentally unbalanced (cf *Smith v M* 1983 SCCR 67; and see 'Insanity' at **2.86**, below).

Dissociation

2.84 It has recently been ruled by the Appeal Court that there is no such defence as 'dissociation' known to Scots law (*Socratous v HM Advocate* 1987 SLT 244 (Note)). What the court seems to have meant is that once a crime has been begun to be perpetrated (a matter fraught with difficulty in relation to offences concerned with the illegal importation of controlled drugs, as in *Socratous*), then all who participate at that point are guilty — either as actors or as art and part. Repentance and attempt to dissociate oneself from the crime are then ineffectual. But, Lord Justice-General Emslie, in delivering the opinion of the court in *Socratous* (at 246) also said this:

'We entirely agree that evidence of "dissociation" by a participant in the preparation of a crime or offence in contemplation will be highly relevant in any decision as to whether he can be held to be in concert with those who proceed to commit it . . .'.

Dissociation then is just one factor to be taken into account in relation to whether a person was art and part guilty of an offence committed by others. As such it may have relevance (if only by way of mitigation) for some forms of breach of the peace, such as those arising from planned (or spontaneous) demonstrations or protest marches.

Error

2.85   Error, or mistake, ought to be as relevant to breach of the peace as it is to any other crime. Thus giving a 'nazi-style' salute (as was *inter alia* originally charged as breach of the peace in *Worsfold v Walkingshaw* 1987 SCCR 17) or a 'pro-Hitler' oration to an audience composed of practising Jews but believed to consist of members of the National Front might provide the occasion for such a defence. The only problem (apart from the evidential one, of course) seems to concern whether such an error has to be a reasonable one as well as being honestly or genuinely held. *Macdonald* (at p 11), founding on *Hume* (vol I, pp 73 & 74) and *Dewar v HM Advocate* (1945 JC 5) asserts that: 'Mistake may also exclude wicked intent, where the mistake is based on reasonable grounds and would, if true, have justified the act done'. But since the last edition of *Macdonald* (5th edn 1948) it has been decided in the case of *Meek v HM Advocate* (1982 SCCR 613) that mistake as to consent in rape is not a matter which requires more than an honest belief (although the greater the unreasonableness of the matter, the less likely it will be that the assertion of 'honest belief' will be accepted). It remains to be seen whether that decision is one confined to rape, or whether it will be applied generally to all errors submitted in defence to criminal charges. However, if it be accepted that *mens rea* is not a particularly relevant consideration in breaches of the peace (see **2.24** to **2.31**, above), and that *Macdonald's* reference to 'wicked intent' is a synonymous expression for *mens rea*, then the applicability of a defence of error to a charge of breach of the peace seems very doubtful. It would only serve to exclude what was not essential in any event (although it may still serve some function *quoad* mitigation. (See also **2.90**, below.)

Insanity

2.86   Insanity at the time of the conduct in question is a good defence to all criminal charges, including those for breaches of the peace (see, for example, *Smith v M* 1983 SCCR 67). If the insanity ('mental disorder' is now a more fashionable appellation) is not spent or is recurrent, then naturally a plea in bar of trial may be considered — although the consequences of doing so must also be considered (Criminal Procedure (Scotland) Act 1975, ss 375, 376(1), (2)). The current Scottish test for insanity which occurred only at the time of the behaviour complained of, is to be deduced from two leading cases (*HM Advocate v Kidd* 1960 JC 61, Lord Strachan's charge to the jury at 70–71, and *Brennan v HM Advocate* 1977 SLT 151, opinion of a full bench at 154). The test involves that the accused should have suffered from a temporary mental defect (arising from mental illness, mental disease, mental defect or unsoundness of mind and *not* from transitory intoxication) which in relation to the act committed amounted to a total alienation of reason (ie which in relation to that act totally prevented him from exercising his reason to exert control over his conduct and reactions). It will be noted that the test is broad (involving not only the above legal test but also consideration of the whole circumstances in the light of common sense). Just what the outcome can be of successfully pleading insanity as a defence to a summary charge of breach of the peace is still in some doubt (see *Renton & Brown* 20-17; *Nicholson* 4-09 to 4-10; *Smith v M*); but there is probably a duty to bring to the court's notice any evidence of mental disorder on the part of the accused (cf *Renton & Brown* at 20-02). The more bizarre forms of conduct giving rise to charges of breach of the peace may in any event suggest mental imbalance. In *Smith v M*, for example, *quoad* the breach of the peace charge, there was a joint minute of admission that the accused had run in front of cars as they passed along a street (forcing them to swerve), torn off his clothing, ripped the exhaust off a taxi in order to belabour the vehicle with it, and so on. It was accepted by both sides that the accused had been insane at the time of that extraordinary conduct, and Sheriff Ireland eventually acquitted him on that basis. (It appeared that since the date of those unfortunate incidents, the accused had been successfully treated for his mental condition. No hospital order of any sort was made.)

Intoxication

2.87   There can be little doubt that self-induced intoxication (whether by drugs or alcohol, or a combination of the two) is not a good defence to a criminal charge. It cannot result in acquittal, and it does not amount to diminished responsibility (these points being made generally by a full bench in the murder case of *Brennan v HM Advocate* 1977 SLT 151). In any event, intoxication can act on criminal responsibility in only two main ways: first, it might prevent one being aware of what one was doing — and that is apparently not a good defence in Scotland (see **2.94**, below), and secondly (and probably additionally), it might prevent the formation of *mens rea* (although *mens rea* may be largely irrelevant *quoad* breach of the peace (see **2.24** to **2.31**, above)). In *Brennan*, however, the view was taken that intoxication may *supply* evidence of *mens rea* (ie where recklessness is sufficient for the crime). A defence based on intoxication, then, would seem to be hopeless — if that intoxication were self-induced. Also, in some cases of breach of the peace, the essence of the charge *is* that the accused was drunk and disorderly. It is, however, just possible that the intoxicatory effects of particular drugs (other than proscribed ones (?)) may be unknown generally and also in particular to the accused; if so, it may be possible (though cf **2.94**, below) for the Scottish courts to be persuaded that English law should be followed and a defence recognised (see *R v Hardie* [1985] 1 WLR 64 — although the general approach of English law to intoxication as a defence is eccentric).

2.88   Whether intoxication can be pled in mitigation will depend on what sort of conduct is involved in the charge. Once again, if the essence of the breach of the peace is that the accused was drunk, it can hardly, one imagines, be a matter of mitigation that he was inebriated. And yet, in some cases, the edge may be taken off the accused's responsibility for that conduct by virtue of his drunkenness. Thus 'deliberate' shouting and swearing at the police to provoke them is one thing; and drunken shouting and swearing in a general, random way is another. There is also some hint in *Hume* (see **1.22** and **1.23**, above) that mitigation in *some* cases may be appropriate. The issue is, however, a narrow one. A drunken man (or woman) is often aggressive and truculent, and all the more alarming than his (or her) sober counterpart simply because of his (or her) intoxicated unpredictability. Whether intoxication can or should be pled in mitigation will depend crucially on the individual facts and circumstances; but in practice it is common to bring to the attention of the court *quantum valeat* the accused's lack of sobriety at the time of the conduct complained of. (It may be thought that *some* explanation offered for the behaviour is better than none at all.) In *James Ainslie* ((1842) 1 Broun 25), on charges of assault, malicious mischief and breach of the peace, the accused's plea of guilty to assault alone was accepted. Evidence that he was intoxicated at the time was also accepted in mitigation by the court. But it should be noted that he had been injured about the head in Australia and had subsequently suffered from 'furiosity' whenever alcohol was ingested. That was not, therefore, a straightforward case. On the other hand, if that case can be made use of as an authority for mitigation, then because it actually involved assault it would be relevant *a fortiori* to breach of the peace.

2.89 Involuntary intoxication may arise in a number of ways. It may arise fortuitously (for example, where there is accidental exposure to noxious fumes), by the intervention of another (as in the 'laced drinks' situation or where consumption is compelled — cf *HM Advocate v Raiker* 1989 SCCR 149), or, by negligence (as, for example, where one fails to notice how much one is actually drinking). How Scots law deals with these different situations is currently uncertain (except in the case of compelled consumption, since in *HM Advocate v Raiker*, Lord McCluskey (at p 154c) told the members of the jury that they might acquit if they found the drug (believed there to be LSD) to have the effect of placing the will of the accused at the disposal of another; but that was so because *mens rea* could not then be inferred on the part of the accused). It is thought, however, that as intoxication leads to a mental state short of insanity and akin (though not amounting) to diminished responsibility, the general effect might be a possible mitigation of sentence (see **2.94**, below, and cf *HM Advocate v Raiker*, Lord McCluskey's opinion at p 155c–d).

2.90 Defences founded on errors which result from intoxication are discredited in England (see, for example, *R v O'Grady* [1987] 3 WLR 321, a case concerning self-defence and the accused's appreciation of the need for it) and there is no reason to suppose that Scots law would adopt any different stance.

Motive

2.91 A 'good' motive is generally discounted as being any defence to a criminal charge. It may be relevant in mitigation of sentence in the same general way that a 'bad' one may be seen as an aggravating circumstance (see **2.75**, above). As much has been specifically held in cases of breach of the peace. In *Deakin v Milne* ((1882) 5 Coup 174), for example, it was argued strongly, at an appeal against conviction for breach of the peace, that Salvation Army marches through the Burgh of Arbroath were both lawful and meritorious, and that any trouble by way of disturbance (or fighting) was at the instance of those evilly opposed to that Army. Lord Justice-Clerk Moncreiff, however, (at 183–4) simply reiterated the general view that the motive of the accused is irrelevant and said: '... [W]here it [ie the procession] leads to breach of the peace, however good the intentions of the person [leading it] may be, the Magistrates are entitled to interfere.' A similar view of the Appeal Court was expressed *a fortiori* in *Palazzo v Copeland* (1976 JC 52). There, at 2 am at the Cross at Stonehouse, youths (in a group) were shouting, swearing and hurling abuse generally in the direction of the accused's house, which was adjacent to the *locus* of the trouble. There was no doubt that the youths' behaviour constituted breach of the peace (some of them later being convicted of that very offence), and the accused decided that the best way of putting an end to their conduct was to fire a shotgun into the air. In so doing, his motive involved the bringing to an end of an existing fracas. This was obviously a 'good' (though somewhat misguided) motive, and it formed the main thrust of the case presented on his behalf at his appeal against conviction for breach of the peace. But the appeal judges would have none of it. However sympathetic the court might have felt towards him, the view was taken that motive was irrelevant to conviction. (It may well be inferential from that decision that the correct time to raise the issue of motive is when sentence is being considered.)

2.92   Before a case of breach of the peace ever proceeds beyond the stage of a police report, it may be that a 'good' motive should be stressed in the course of informal discussions with the procurator fiscal. This could lead to the dropping of charges, or to the adoption of some more favourable alternative to prosecution (for example, a warning letter (see 1979 SLT (News) 279) or a 'fiscal' fine — see the Criminal Justice (Scotland) Act 1987, s 56), since prosecutors should weigh any excuse tendered for the suspect's conduct in arriving at a decision whether prosecution in the public interest would be justified (see *Renton & Brown* 3-01).

Necessity

2.93 It is not at all clear that Scots law recognises any general defence of necessity. It is further not clear what necessity means. (For a general discussion of these problems, see T Jones, *The Defence of Necessity in Scots Law*, 1989 SLT (News) 253.) Typically in academic writings, necessity is identified with 'natural' (as opposed to third-party, human) pressures which dictate the making of some decision involving breach of the law. Presumably hunger (or any other basic human need requiring satisfaction for the maintenance of life) is such a natural pressure. Certainly it forms the basis of *Hume's* discussion of the issue (I, p 55–56); and if it be that the pressing need for food is rejected in relation to theft (as it is by Hume), there would seem little room for any defence of necessity. In the sheriff court case of *Tudhope v Grubb* (1983 SCCR 350), necessity was *ex facie* the reason for an acquittal on a charge of attempting to drive a motor vehicle with more than the permitted level of alcohol in the accused's body. But there were third-party human beings creating pressures for the accused. (The accused had been attacked by others and had entered his car in a 'drunken' state in an endeavour to make his escape.) The decision is partly, therefore, consistent with a defence of coercion (though differing from that defence in that the assailants did not require the accused to perform in the way that he did) as also with self-defence (since it is a requirement of self-defence that one should endeavour to escape one's attacker, if one can, rather than resort to counter-violence). The case, therefore, is of little authority *quoad* necessity. (It is also only a sheriff court decision.) *Palazzo v Copeland* (1976 JC 52) might have provided the occasion for an investigation of necessity, in that the accused could have argued that by firing a shotgun in the air, he was vindicating a form of public necessity in that the fracas in the street below him was disturbing the peace of the community and immediate action was necessary to bring it to an end. But presumably the police could have been summoned instead, and it did not seem that the conduct of the youths (shouting and swearing) was so unusual or immediately threatening to life, limb or property as to require instant action at the hands of the accused. In any event, no defence of necessity was tendered, and no comment was made by the Appeal Court on that issue. There seems no good reason, however, why circumstances approaching typical necessity should not be tendered (at least) in mitigation of sentence for breach of the peace. They might also be brought to the attention of fiscals at the stage of informal discussions *quoad* a projected prosecution (for the reasons stated at **2.92**, above).

Non-insane automatism

2.94   It is not a defence leading to acquittal that the accused was
unaware of what he was doing at the time due to some mental
condition (not satisfying the test for insanity — see **2.86**, above) or the
effect of some disease (as, for example, diabetes — *Carmichael v Boyle*
1985 SCCR 58). Such unawareness may, however, amount to *de facto*
diminished responsibility (see **2.83**, above) and lead to mitigation of
sentence after conviction. Although the leading authority on this
matter did not involve breach of the peace, and indeed involved a
certified matter in solemn proceedings (*HM Advocate v Cunningham*
1963 JC 80), that authority has been specifically confirmed in *Carmichael v Boyle*. There, the second of the five charges in the complaint
read that the accused did conduct himself 'in a disorderly manner,
shout, swear, use obscene and abusive language and commit a breach
of the peace'. Boyle was in fact a sufferer from an unstable form of
diabetes which required very strict control. Regular injections of
insulin had to be balanced by regular intake of food; and the ingestion
of alcohol was frowned upon, since it had the effect of upsetting the
delicate balance of the accused's condition. Sheriff Boyle found that
the accused was of unusually low intelligence and that he thus had
difficulty in adhering to his strict regime. (Failure to adhere to it
would result in the rapid onset of hypoglycaemia, the outward mani-
festation of which being irrational, and in some cases violent behaviour of which the sufferer would probably not be aware.) On the day in
question, the accused had his doses of insulin but little food. He also
drank several pints of beer. In the ensuing hypoglycaemic state, he
committed (*inter alia*) the breach of the peace mentioned above. The
medical evidence painted a picture of involuntary behaviour stem-
ming from a mental or pathological state not amounting to insanity.
(It may be noted that Sheriff Boyle (at 64) opined that the accused
might have pled legal insanity but had chosen not to do so. It would be
difficult, however, to reconcile that view with the accepted Scottish
test for insanity — see **2.86**, above.) The sheriff clearly had much
sympathy for the accused's plight and strove to distinguish *HM
Advocate v Cunningham* (which appeared to require conviction) by
confining it to crimes not requiring *mens rea*. (This argument made
sense in relation to the assault with which Boyle was also charged, but
seemed counter-productive *quoad* breach of the peace — see **2.31**,
above.) As the Crown, in these circumstances, had not according to
the sheriff satisfied the court of the existence of *mens rea*, an acquittal
of *all* charges was the inevitable result. The Crown appealed and won
the ruling it sought from the High Court, viz. that the decision in *HM
Advocate v Cunningham* was perfectly general and allowed a person

such as Boyle mitigation of sentence only. This, therefore, would appear to rule out any hope of a non-insane automatism defence (except in mitigation) in response to breach of the peace. But it should be noted that Boyle's defence was undermined in several ways. In particular, low intelligence or not, he had often been in a hypogly-caemic state and had often as a result exhibited violent and aggressive behaviour — of which he could hardly have been unaware; he had also voluntarily consumed alcohol on the day in question (thus effecting the frowned-upon state of self-induced intoxication — see **2.87** ff, above); and, before the Appeal Court, his counsel conceded that he could support neither Sheriff Boyle's reasoning nor the acquittal. This is not to suggest that the outcome in *Carmichael v Boyle* was wrong in law or even in general; but it can thus be demonstrated that Boyle's position was far weaker than it is often represented to have been. If the decision in *HM Advocate v Cunningham* is felt to be unjust because of its sweeping generality, then a far stronger case would have been necessary to merit the attentions of a full bench — that now being the only conceivable (non-statutory) way of altering *Cunningham's* ratio.

Prevention of illegal activity

2.95   It is not a defence to a charge of breach of the peace that the conduct was done to prevent the carrying out, or continuance, of some other crime or unlawful activity. In *Palazzo v Copeland* (1976 JC 52), for example, it was held on appeal not to be a defence that the accused committed a breach of the peace in an effort to stop an existing breach of the peace. Lord Justice-General Emslie in delivering the opinion of the court said (at 54): 'A man may not take the law into his own hands. Furthermore a man may not commit an offence in an attempt to stop another.' In other words, one will not be acquitted of breach of the peace on such a plea; but it does not follow that that sort of plea is totally irrelevant. Indeed, there is fair authority for the view that it may be considered relevant at the point of sentence, after conviction. Even in *Palazzo v Copeland*, the fine imposed was a small one of £25. Nineteenth century authority, however, makes the point more direct-ly. In *McDonald v Mackay* ((1842) 1 Broun 435), the accused were charged with mobbing and rioting, breach of the peace, and malicious mischief in that they had assembled for the purposes of tearing down toll gates and the prevention of the collection of tolls, and indeed had succeeded in doing both. They were convicted (after a sheriff and jury trial) of malicious mischief and breach of the peace, and appealed to a circuit court on the ground that the sheriff had refused to receive evidence that the toll gates had been erected in the wrong place, were not statutorily authorised, and hence were unlawful. The circuit court quashed their convictions, holding that at the very least the accused should have been allowed to lead evidence of the toll gates' illegality in 'alleviation' (ie mitigation) if not in exculpation. That the prevention of alleged unlawfulness is not an exculpatory matter can be strengthened by reference to *Thomas Wild* ((1854) 1 Irv 552) where the charges were mobbing and rioting and assault on facts very similar to those in *McDonald v Mackay*. As Lord Cowan said to the jury (at 557–8):

'From the remarks of one of the counsel, you may have been led to believe that the levying of the toll in this case was illegal, and that this formed a certain justification of the proceedings . . . but . . . be the exaction legal or illegal, no one is entitled, irrespectively of the judgments of the law courts, by force or masterful means, to prevent the exaction of a toll . . . The remedy is, to go to the courts of law, and when it is fixed that the toll is no longer exigible, then the civil power can be called in to prevent the Trustees from exacting any more toll.'

The accused were then convicted in various ways of the offences libelled, but the maximum prison sentence imposed was six months — rather less than would have been anticipated in relation to contemporary mobbing and rioting convictions which exhibited no mitigating features. A slightly more modern authority may be quoted to the same end. The charges in *HM Advocate v Gollan* ((1883) 5 Coup 317) concerned mobbing and rioting, assault and breach of the peace. The accused were convicted of mobbing and rioting only, but the jury recommended that clemency be exercised due to their 'ignorance of the law and strong religious convictions'. The accused had formed part of a crowd of persons (nearly 200 strong) which had taken forceful steps to prevent Sunday landings of fish at Strome ferry. Their object had been to prevent desecration of the Sabbath — ie prevention of an unlawful activity, as they saw it. Lord Justice-Clerk Moncreiff had told the jury (at 323–4) that the accuseds' supposed upholding of the Scottish strict sabbatarian 'laws' was not a plea in exculpation, since the proper remedy was to fight their case in the civil courts and not on the quayside at Strome. Were it otherwise, then there would exist a recipe for anarchy — with persons free to try to uphold by force whatever they considered to be the correct position in law (and he mentioned in particular by way of illustration the 'Salvation Army case' — surely *Deakin v Milne* ((1882) 5 Coup 174) — where the Salvationists and their rivals (the Skeleton Army) had fought, each in pretended vindication of the 'rightness' of their respective views of the law). After conviction, however, the Lord

Justice-Clerk affirmed (at 327) that such 'ignorance of the law' (ie of how to vindicate their perception of breach of the law) could be taken account of at sentence, in mitigation; and the prison sentences imposed were a 'lenient' four months.

Provocation

2.96   Retaliatory violence constituting an assault may be regarded as a lesser degree of assault because of provocation. As some forms of breach of the peace border upon assault (see **2.78**, above), it seems to follow that provocation can operate here also, and in a similar way (ie it will not exculpate but may serve to mitigate). There is a dearth of authority, however, on the effect of this mitigatory plea in relation to breach of the peace. Nevertheless, the practice is to lead evidence of provocation *quantum valeat*; and such practice was not treated as incompetent in *Gallocher v Weir and Patrick* ((1902) 3 Adam 665). The complaint there charged a typical form of breach of the peace involving violence — viz. that the accused behaved in a disorderly manner, cursed, swore, quarrelled and fought, annoyed the lieges and committed a breach of the peace. The defence of provocation had been raised, one of the accused having argued that he had been subject to sustained verbal provocation from his co-accused. Indeed, he alleged that he had often been sworn at and threatened, and had offered to show that provocative words had been uttered on 28 February (the alleged offence having been committed on 7 March). On appeal against conviction, this issue was argued afresh on his behalf, but Lord Justice-Clerk Macdonald (at 667) stated: 'It is a fixed principle of our criminal law that it is not competent in a criminal case to appeal to provocation caused by words uttered several days before the crime took place.' Lords Young and Trayner concurred in that statement of the law, as well they might since it follows *Hume's* assessment of verbal provocation (I, pp 333–4). But the important and relevant conclusion does not concern whether provocation is possible by words, nor whether 'cumulative provocation' is here rejected (both issues of current interest to commentators on the criminal law — see, for example, *Gane & Stoddart*, pp 526–535); the significant point is that the court did not exclude provocation on the grounds that it was irrelevant to breach of the peace. (It should be noted, however, that provocation may have been pled in that case as (and treated by the court as if it were) a defence capable of leading to exculpation, since confusion as to its true role was rife until comparatively recent years — see *Fenning v HM Advocate* 1985 SLT 540. But if the court was so treating provocation, then surely the finding that it was not irrelevant to breach of the peace even on that basis is a powerful argument for its reception as a mere mitigatory plea.)

Self-defence

2.97   Self-defence is an exculpatory plea relevant to assault and to homicide. In so far as some forms of conduct sufficient for breach of the peace are close to assault (see **2.78**, above), then self-defence should also be applicable to the 'lesser offence' (as Lord Murray, dissenting, referred to breach of the peace vis-à-vis assault in *Butcher v Jessop* 1989 SCCR 119 at 134G to 135A). Henry H Brown ('Breach of the Peace' (1895) 3 SLT 151 and 163 at 165) certainly thought that that was so, although it is difficult to find reported cases of breach of the peace in which it has genuinely featured. In *Butcher v Jessop*, it was argued before the sheriff court that a charge of breach of the peace in the standard statutory form of 'disorderly conduct' (see **2.02**, above) gave insufficient notice of the case the Crown intended to prove. The point was that the Crown intended to prove violent conduct verging upon assault on the parts of the accused, and the accused in turn argued that that was not the sort of 'breach of the peace' that they had prepared themselves to meet. What, in particular, since the case against them was apparently tantamount to assault, of the possible defence of self-defence? The learned sheriff (though not conceding that the accused were (or even could be) ignorant of the sort of case they had to meet) offered an adjournment so that evidence in respect of self-defence might be prepared (see 124E–F, and 125B–C). That offer was not taken up; but the interesting conclusion is that the sheriff did not consider that self-defence could not be pled in response to that sort of breach of the peace. (Unfortunately, at the later Appeal Court hearing, there was no discussion of self-defence in relation to the offence.)

2.98   It may be possible to argue in an appropriate case of breach of the peace that a form of 'self-defence' — in the wide aspect of defence of self and one's property — may apply. This could arise as a tentative inference from the decision in *Palazzo v Copeland* (1976 JC 52). There the accused had fired a gun into the air from a window of his house in order to put a stop to an existing breach of the peace in the street outside. The disturbance in question was being caused by youths who were only momentarily cowed by the accused's actions and who shortly afterwards resumed and escalated their misbehaviour. In particular they then broke a window of the accused's house and also damaged his car. As the Appeal Court set some store by the sequence of those events, it may be possible to argue that the outcome might have been different had the youths 'assaulted' the accused's property prior to his discharging his shotgun. If no immediate help was at hand, should the owner have had to stand by whilst his property was quickly destroyed by the actions of persons such as the youths in *Palazzo v Copeland*? If this is thought to place too great a premium on defending *property*, the argument could be refined by reference to the distinct possibility that the youths might have followed their acts of damage by an assault on the owner of the house (especially since there had been previous trouble caused by youths, in respect of which the owner might have lodged complaints with the police). Such an extended view of self-defence is, however, extremely tentative.

Sports

2.99   There is no doubt that breach of the peace can be charged in respect of incidents which take place in the course of playing a physical contact sport (*Butcher v Jessop* 1989 SCCR 119). Physical contact sports are many and varied, but would obviously include team sports (such as football, rugby, shinty, hockey, netball, cricket (?), and water-polo) and also individual contests (such as are involved in judo, karate, boxing, wrestling and fencing). Although it is possible to envisage the type of breach of the peace which involves only those playing the sport and that *inter se* (for example, one player shouting and swearing at, and repeatedly threatening, members of the opposing team), the more usual case is predicated upon the effect of players' behaviour on those watching the match or contest. Especially in the case of large-crowd sporting events (for example, premier league football matches), there will inevitably in any event be excitement, tension and rivalry between or amongst the different groups of supporters. All 'recognised' physical contact sports (cf the 'square go' referred to in *Smart v HM Advocate* 1975 JC 30) also have rules which specify the object of the game, how that object is to be attained during play, and what is to be done if players infringe those rules in various pre-considered ways. Most sports also have referees, part of whose task is to 'police' the field of play and to operate the rules in relation to infringements. Again where teams are involved in playing the sport, each side will have a captain, part of whose duty is concerned with 'policing' his team and upholding his team's cause if infringements of the rules are indulged in by his opponents. Obviously too, when one side (or individual) achieves the object of play (eg scoring a goal) within the rules, this will often generate great excitement on the part of its or his supporters (and corresponding wrath on the part of the opposing team or individual's supporters). But reaction or adverse reaction on the part of onlookers to what takes place legitimately within the rules of the sport cannot constitute a breach of the peace on the part of players or participants on the field of play, the boxing-ring, the swimming-pool, or whatever. If there be breach of the peace in such a situation, that is the responsibility of the onlookers themselves. (There may be one exception to this in a case where disturbance was highly likely by playing the game at all. If, for example, a Scottish football team were to play an invitation match against a visiting South African team, and if it could be shown that opponents of the South African political regime had done their best to disrupt similar matches in the recent past, it is just possible that the teams or their managers could be charged with breach of the peace by insisting on playing in the face of an obviously hostile crowd and against the advice of the authorities. It is not clear either that the exclusion of the public from the stadium in question would be a complete answer. Such a charge in such circumstances seems unlikely, however, in practice (but cf *Deakin v Milne* (1882) 5 Coup 174).)

2.100   Much more difficult is the question of incidents between or among players during play where those incidents have nothing to do with the legitimate objects of the sport. Of these, some may be catered for by the rules (eg in football, making a very late tackle or handling the ball); but others may be beyond what the rules could possibly envisage (eg one player kicking another to death). Where the circumstances in relation to the onlookers are already highly volatile (eg at a Rangers–Celtic football match, where the crowds of supporters represent rivalries not only in sport but also in religious belief), it might be argued that any incident, whether within the rules relating to infringements or beyond them, which produces (or might reasonably produce) the requisite result on the part of the crowd (or a section of the crowd) — ie disturbance, fighting, annoyance, invasion of the pitch, and so on — should be regarded as a breach of the peace on the part of the players responsible. This was not quite the approach taken, however, in the leading case of *Butcher v Jessop*. There, during a Rangers–Celtic football match before a crowd of 43,000, the goalkeeper and captain for one side visited a player from the opposing side with violence over a mere seven-second period when play had temporarily ceased. The crowd reacted adversely to an extent (and might reasonably have reacted adversely to a far greater extent). The two who had been responsible for the violence on the field were consequently convicted of breach of the peace because of the effect which their conduct had, or might reasonably have had, on the crowd in the circumstances — an effect which they ought to have anticipated. In relation to the accused who had captained his side, Sheriff Mackay (at 123A) found that his actings 'were unjustified by the rules of the game, his duties as captain, the heat of the contest in the course of a vigorous contact sport, or any other factors'. With respect to the accused goalkeeper's actions, there was a similar finding, save for the deletion (of course) of any reference to the duties of a team captain. At their later appeals against conviction, Lord Justice-Clerk Ross (with whom Lord Allanbridge concurred) accepted (at 130F–G) that the sheriff, by making these findings 'clearly had regard to the fact that this incident took place in the context of a game of football . . . [and] that the actings of the first appellant [the team captain] could not be justified or excused as being a normal incident in a game of football'. (A similar statement was made by the Lord Justice-Clerk in relation to the actings of the goalkeeper — see 133D).

2.101   The importance of the decision in *Butcher v Jessop, quoad* such allegations of breach of the peace, is that it would seem to be a defence that what a player did (notwithstanding the effect of that on the onlookers) was in furtherance of the duties expected of him as a team captain bearing in mind the rules of the sport, or was done in the course of the excitement generated by the contest or game itself. Thus, a team captain on the football field might be justified in forcibly separating two players who had come to blows; and a boxer might be excused for throwing a foul punch during the violent tension of a boxing match. Naturally too, any other defence normally available to one charged with breach of the peace will apply in relation to incidents on the sports field. A player who is visited with violence by another is, for example, surely entitled to defend himself. But in the factual absence of any onlookers at all (the public having been excluded, for example, or preferring to watch the contest on television at home), it is impossible to envisage any success attending the type of prosecution brought in *Butcher v Jessop*. The incident involved in that case could, one supposes, have caused *de facto* disturbance in many Glasgow homes if the match had been screened on a television channel. But such disturbance would be so indirectly and non-immediately related to the conduct as to be beyond the reach of breach of the peace.

Taking precautions to avoid disturbance or annoyance

2.102 '[T]he question is whether breach of the peace should be so defined that it can be committed by a man who has deliberately and successfully taken proper precautions to prevent any breach of the public peace, and it is submitted that it should not be so defined.' This submission (by the anonymous author of the article 'Breach of the Peace', 1959 SLT (News) 229 at 232), if accepted by the courts, would seem to raise a defence of having taken all reasonable precautions to avoid one's behaviour bringing about a proscribed result relative to breach of the peace. The case which the author was thinking of, however, was that of *Young v Heatly* (1959 JC 66). It is thought that that is not the best of authorities to pray in aid, since the precautions which the depute headmaster took there (ie speaking to boys in the privacy of his own room behind a closed door) looked suspicious rather than well intentioned in view of his design to make indecent remarks to students to whom he stood virtually *in loco parentis* (and in respect of whom he could have had no clear idea whether or not they shared his sexual mores). Indeed, if the case be considered as virtually one of shamelessly indecent conduct (see **2.43**, above), then the precautions he took, in the circumstances of what he had to say, would have reinforced the inference of *mens rea* rather than provided him with a defence (see *Robertson v Smith* 1980 JC 1).

2.103 It would certainly, however, be an attractive proposition in an appropriate case that the accused had taken reasonable precautions to avoid (say) annoying others. Thus, a compulsive 'curser and swearer' might seek out an apparently deserted and isolated quarry in which to give vent to his vocabulary, not knowing (and having no reason to suspect) that some bird watchers were concealed for their own purposes nearby (though that might attract perhaps the defence of 'accident') or that he was being zealously followed by two private detectives hired by his spouse (who had suspected him of infidelity). Whether a defence of 'all reasonable precautions' would prevail in such circumstances has not featured directly in any breach of the peace case, but something akin to it may lie behind the quashing of the conviction in *Thompson v MacPhail* (1989 SCCR 266). There the accused had locked himself into a toilet cubicle in order to inject himself with some unknown substance. Suspicion was aroused, at least in the mind of the manager of the 'Fast Burger' premises in question, because of the length of time that the accused was occupying the cubicle. The police were called, and the door was unlocked from the outside. The accused was then seen by two police officers and the manager. He was caught in the act of withdrawing a syringe from his arm. There was blood on the floor and wall. There was no struggle or *de facto* disturbance of any kind. It was quite obvious that the accused had done his best to conceal what he was doing from the attentions of any other human being and that he had taken precautions to avoid alarm or annoyance (or whatever) to others. In quashing the appellant's conviction for breach of the peace, Lord Brand drew attention to the lack of precise information as to how long he had been in the cubicle and as to the likely demand from other customers for use of that cubicle, and concluded (at 268D):

'It is therefore impossible to say whether or not anything that occurred as a result of a customer remaining inside a cubicle was likely to cause the privacy of the cubicle to be invaded and the conduct of the person inside the cubicle to become exposed and to be likely to cause alarm to the lieges.'

It is arguable, therefore, that the question truly at issue in that case was — 'how reasonable (on an objective basis) were the precautions adopted by the accused to avoid alarm or annoyance (or whatever) being caused to others by his conduct?' 'Reasonable' there would probably mean 'effective' — given all the relevant circumstances of the case.

Arrest without warrant

2.104 Subsequent case law has affirmed *Hume's* view (see **1.21**, above), and thus 'a constable is entitled to arrest, without a warrant, any person seen by him committing a breach of the peace, and he may arrest on the direct evidence of eye-witnesses'. (*Jackson v Stevenson* (1897) 24 R (J) 38 at 40, per Lord Justice-General Robertson; as approved in *Adair v McGarry* 1933 JC 72 at 78, per Lord Justice-General Clyde and at 89, per Lord Morison.) It may possibly be more realistic, however, to state that a constable may arrest any person he *reasonably* suspects to be committing a breach of the peace. He may also, in respect of such suspicion, exercise the powers of detention found in section 2 of the Criminal Justice (Scotland) Act 1980, breach of the peace being a common law crime and thus 'an offence punishable by imprisonment'.

Words

2.105 Some words, commonly used by the courts in relation to breach of the peace, may require some little elaboration. Even the word 'peace' itself seems somewhat mysterious given the wide range of conduct which is regarded as falling within the four corners of the offence. In *Ferguson v Carnochan* (see Appendix), Lord McLaren was at pains to dispel any suggestion that breach of the 'peace' was only commensurate with brawling and fighting, and in one version of his speech (2 White 278 at 281) said: 'The term peace is not used as the antithesis of war'. And indeed the Shorter Oxford English Dictionary provides several significances of the word quite apart from 'freedom from war or hostilities', viz: freedom from civil commotion; public order or security; freedom from disturbance or perturbation; quiet; tranquillity; freedom from quarrel or dissension; freedom from mental or spiritual disturbance; and, absence of noise, movement or activity. Most of these would be consistent with the case decisions pertaining to the offence, in its 'disturbance of the standing peace of the *locus*' form, and at least one of them (ie freedom from mental or spiritual disturbance) with the 'alarm, annoyance or other mental trauma' form (see **2.23**, above, as also **2.107**, below). Nineteenth century charges very often specifically referred to breach of the 'public' peace, but the epithet 'public' is now thought superfluous, and is very rarely encountered.

2.106   In many reported cases, from the nineteenth century to the present, it is stated that the accused's conduct was 'calculated' to produce some result required by the offence. In *Dougall v Dykes* ((1861) 4 Irv 101), for example, Lord Justice-Clerk Inglis said (at 106) that 'such conduct was directly calculated to produce a breach of the peace', whereas Lord Neaves stated (at 105): 'The conduct . . . was calculated to give rise to great irritation, and to a determination to repress it'. Again, in *Raffaelli v Heatly* (1949 JC 101), Lord Mackay's opinion contained the following: 'If acts are repeated and are calculated to cause alarm and annoyance, I think that is enough'. In these two cases, it is possible (and could have been consistent with the facts) that the accused had intended to disturb or to alarm and annoy; but since it is plain that the judges in question were referring to something essential for conviction (and since *mens rea* in the form of intention is certainly not a *sine qua non* for conviction of breach of the peace, see **2.25**, above), 'calculated' must mean something different from 'intended'. The meaning to be assigned must also make sense in relation to Lord Justice-General Emslie's statement (in *Palazzo v Copeland* 1976 JC 52 at 53) that 'the act of firing a gun in the air in an urban situation at that time in the morning was calculated to be likely to put lieges in general in a state of fear and alarm'. From the several possibilities to be found in the OED (1933 edn), the meaning which will best fit the various *dicta* above is thought to be this — 'of a nature or character' (rather than the simpler 'likely'). Whether or not the accused's conduct was of the requisite 'nature or character' will obviously depend on all the circumstances; but it will be determined objectively.

2.107 From at least the time when *Ferguson v Carnochan* ((1889) 2 White 278) was decided, the word 'decorum' has been used in relation to breach of the peace. As interpreted in *Raffaelli v Heatly* (1949 JC 101, see **2.20**, above), Lord McLaren's opinion in *Ferguson v Carnochan* considered breach of the peace to involve a breach of 'public order' (see the definitions of 'peace' at **2.105**, above) *or* 'decorum'. What he meant by 'decorum' is of some importance, since that word is still commonly encountered in relation to breach of the peace. Once again, the OED (1933 edn) provides a variety of significances; but bearing in mind the types of case in which it is used, 'decorum' must mean 'propriety of behaviour', 'what is fitting or proper in behaviour or demeanour', or 'what is in conformity to the recognised standards of propriety and good taste in manners, behaviour, etc.' This would seem to underline yet again that breach of the peace has been conflated with offences in breach of the public police (see **1.17** to **1.20**, above) in modern times.

Sentence issues

2.108 Sentencing issues in relation to breach of the peace are really no different from those *quoad* other offences, save that breach of the peace is generally considered a minor crime (see **2.08** ff, above) and that prison ought, therefore, to be used sparingly. Of course, being a common law crime, breach of the peace undeniably carries a possible prison sentence (see *Orr v McCallum* (1855) 2 Irv 183 at 196, per Lord Justice-General McNeill) up to the limit of the powers of the sentencing court. But in *Kelly v Rowan* ((1897) 2 Adam 357) Lord Justice-Clerk Macdonald (at 361) opined that seven days in prison would be a severe penalty for breach of the peace, unless there were aggravations (see **2.70** ff, above). Fines, caution, probation or community service are generally the preferred disposals here, unless there are significant previous convictions (eg *Quinn v Wilson* 1989 GWD 17-729; *McCorkell v Wilson* 1989 GWD 6-249), or a conviction for breach of the peace *per se* has emerged from an indictment which originally charged more (typically mobbing and rioting — eg *Michael Currie* (1864) 4 Irv 578; *HM Advocate v Blair* (1868) 1 Coup 168), or there are aggravations (see **2.70** ff, above). It may be, however, that a conviction for certain types of breach of the peace may carry a latent additional 'penalty', in the form of revocation of a shotgun or firearm certificate (cf *Luke v*

Little 1980 SLT (Sh Ct) 138, where the sheriff confirmed that revocation of a shotgun certificate was justified in the case of a person convicted for the third time of an offence under s 6(1) of the Road Traffic Act 1972 — now s 5(1) of the Road Traffic Act 1988 — the issue being that that person's proven irresponsibility with his car might easily be translated into irresponsibility with a shotgun). The grant of such a certificate may also be prejudiced, since a chief constable must be satisfied that the applicant can have such a weapon 'without danger to the public safety or to the peace'. (See the Firearms Act 1968, ss 27, 28 and 30, as amended by the Firearms (Amendment) Act 1988.)

III   Conduct and results

Results

3.01   Although breach of the peace is a result crime (see **2.23**, above), no particular result need be specified in a complaint. The standard, statutory styles of charge do not show any particular result (see **2.02**, above), and where those styles are employed without elaboration, the court in question would be free to find any recognised result in order to proceed to conviction (see, for example, *Shannon v Skeen* (1977) SCCR Supp 180, where the sheriff found in fact that there had been reasonable alarm caused by persistent following). A court could indeed make a finding of alarm, annoyance, concern, danger, distress, disturbance, embarrassment, fear, obstruction, shock, temptation to make reprisals, terror, or upset — real (if reasonable) or reasonably to be anticipated, whichever seemed appropriate in relation to the proven (or admitted) conduct. (It should be noted that it is not entirely certain that each of these would be sufficient *per se*, since some have not been specifically tested in the Appeal Court.) The Crown does, however, even today, sometimes libel a specific result (or specific results). Where it does, then presumably conviction cannot follow unless that result (or those results) can be shown. In such cases, the matter of result is no longer at large.

Alarm

3.02   One of the oldest recorded results is alarm (see **1.05**, above), and it is still common to find it expressed in complaints for breach of the peace (see, for example, *Palazzo v Copeland* 1976 JC 52 — discharging a shotgun into the air 'to the alarm of the lieges'; *Marshall v MacDougall* 1986 SCCR 376 — bawling, cursing and adopting a threatening attitude 'and by such behaviour place him and [two others] all in a state of alarm'). It may also be found in association with others. 'Alarm and annoyance' is commonly enough found (eg *Peter Jefferson & George Forbes* (1848) Arkley 464, *quoad* the prior charge of breach of the peace against them, claimed to be in bar of the (then) present trial; *Ferguson v Carnochan* (1889) 2 White 278; *Fisher v Keane* 1981 JC 50), as is that the 'victim' was put into 'a state of fear and alarm' (eg *Raffaelli v Heatly* 1949 JC 101; *Taylor v Hamilton* 1984 SCCR 393). *Hume* also referred to 'alarm and disturbance' (see **1.05**, above). Sometimes too, the 'alarm' will be stated as a general one shared by the lieges (eg *Palazzo v Copeland; Tudhope v O'Neill* 1983 SCCR 443) or the 'neighbourhood' (eg *Peter Jefferson & George Forbes*). But it is also possible to libel the 'alarm' of a particular individual or group (eg *Armour v Macrae* (1886) 1 White 58 — the chairman of, and certain parties at, a political meeting; *Raffaelli v Heatly* — the residents of a particular Edinburgh street; *Benson v Tudhope* 1986 SCCR 422 — a 15-year-old girl and four women; *Marshall v MacDougall* — three boys of 14, 16, and 17 years of age; *Mackie v MacLeod* (March 1961, unreported) High Court — see *Gordon* at p 488 — the female half of a couple of persons who were persistently followed).

3.03   What 'alarm' means *quoad* breach of the peace was discussed in the late nineteenth century case of *Ferguson v Carnochan* ((1889) 2 White 278 — see Appendix). According to Lord Justice-Clerk Macdonald, it could mean fear for one's personal safety (and this, it is suggested, is what it usually will mean when specific persons are said to be 'alarmed') provided that such fear is reasonable, given the conduct and the circumstances, or reasonable fear that there is, or will be, disturbance of the standing peace of the *locus* if the conduct is permitted to continue (which is what will usually be meant if it is the lieges in general who are, or the neighbourhood which is, said to be 'alarmed'). Fear of temptation to make reprisals may also be contained within the term 'alarm' (eg *Mackie v MacLeod* (March 1961 unreported) High Court — see *Gordon* at p 488); *Raffaelli v Heatly* 1949 JC 101). If none of these can be shown, then a complaint which specifies 'alarm' will surely fail to result in a conviction (eg *Armour v Macrae* (1886) 1 White 58).

Annoyance

3.04   It is rare to find 'annoyance' as the only result specified in a complaint for breach of the peace (cf *Peter Phillips & William Ford v John Cross* (1848) J Shaw 139, where the charge concluded — 'and also did conduct themselves otherwise in a riotous and disorderly manner to the annoyance of the lieges and in breach of the peace'). Much more common is to find it in combination with others, particularly 'alarm' (see **3.02**, above), 'disturbance' (eg *Matthews & Rodden v*

Linton (1860) 3 Irv 570 — 'whereby the lieges were annoyed and disturbed'; *Whitchurch v Millar* (1895) 2 Adam 9 — 'and annoyed and disturbed the lieges'); 'terror' (eg *MacDougall v Maclullich* (1887) 1 White 328 — 'to the great terror, annoyance and alarm of the lieges'); 'molestation' (eg *Sleigh & Russell v Moxey* (1850) J Shaw 369 — 'whereby the chairman and those present were annoyed and molested'); and 'distress' (eg *Turner v Kennedy* (1972) SCCR Supp 30 — 'which did cause annoyance and distress'). That being so, it is a matter for consideration whether 'annoyance' *per se* is a sufficient result for conviction. In *Ferguson v Carnochan* ((1889) 2 White 278) where the complaint had specified both 'alarm' and 'annoyance', Lord Justice-Clerk Macdonald stated (but in the '2 White' version only, at p 280 — see Appendix):

'And I do not doubt that sober and reasonably minded people might be seriously annoyed by a disturbance such as is set forth in this case, being continued, and that it was a disturbance of the public peace.'

This suggests, but no more, that *serious* annoyance on the part of ordinary people would be sufficient. Some support for the sufficiency of simple 'annoyance', on the other hand, can be found in Lord Young's opinion in *Whitchurch v Millar* (at 12) where he conceded that there had been no violence involved in the case, but drew attention to the fact that there had been 'annoyance', and that the magistrates (of Hamilton) had been entitled to stop the procession in question and to prosecute for breach of the peace those who persisted in holding it. Again, in *Donaghy v Tudhope* (1985 SCCR 118) where no specific result was contained in the complaint, the sheriff made a finding that men, who could not work on a building site because of the accuseds' actions (climbing tower cranes as a 'peace protest'), were 'annoyed', in order to justify (partly, at least) his conclusion that the offence had been committed. On the basis of these decisions, the most that can be said is that 'annoyance' *per se* may be a sufficient result.

3.05 'Annoyance' can be expressed both in general terms — as being caused to the lieges (eg *McGuire v Fairbairn* (1881) 4 Coup 536; *MacDougall v Maclullich* (1887) 1 White 328) or a particular group of persons (eg *Dougall v Dykes* (1861) 4 Irv 101 — the minister and congregation of East Kilbride parish church; *Sleigh & Russell v Moxey* (1850) J Shaw 369 — the chairman and those present at a meeting) — and in relation to specific, named individuals (eg *Turner v Kennedy* (1972) SCCR Supp 30 — the persons named in a schedule attached to the complaint). Where individuals are concerned, it will obviously be necessary for the prosecutor to show that they were in fact annoyed and that that had been a reasonable response on their parts to the conduct. But it is not all clear what 'annoyance' means in the context of breach of the peace. It is clearly a weaker mental state than 'alarm'; but few of the cases discuss its exact significance. In the anonymous article 'Breach of the Peace' (1959 SLT (News) 229 at 230), it is suggested that the verb 'to annoy' means to irritate (cf *Dougall v Dykes*, opinion of Lord Neaves at 105) or to arouse disapproval. But it is thought that more than that should be required, to the point of the 'seriousness' apparently specified by Lord Justice-Clerk Macdonald in *Ferguson v Carnochan* (see **3.04**, above), and perhaps to the point where there arises 'a determination to repress' the conduct (cf *Dougall v Dykes*, Lord Neave's opinion, at 105). Any finding of 'annoyance' must, of course, be one which is reasonable given the conduct and the circumstances.

Concern

3.06   In the case of *Turner v Kennedy* ((1972) SCCR Supp 30), on a complaint for breach of the peace which libelled only annoyance *and* distress caused to particular individuals, it was found in the burgh court that some of the individuals had indeed been annoyed *or* distressed by the conduct, but that others were alarmed by it, and that one of them had been 'concerned'. As an appeal against conviction was simply dismissed by the High Court (which did not deliver opinions), it is not clear what weight ought to be given to 'concern'. It seems to have been a superfluous finding in fact, and gives no real basis for convicting solely on such a result. No guidance was given on what 'concern' might mean, and, therefore, its ordinary meaning would presumably apply. (See also *McMillan v Normand* 1989 SCCR 269, where 'concern' may have been equated with 'alarm or annoyance'.) Presumably also both individuals and the lieges in general could be 'concerned' in relation to some sufficient conduct.

Danger

3.07   Occasionally in charges for breach of the peace, references are found to the lieges 'being put in danger' (eg *Cochran v Ferguson* (1882) 5 Coup 169) or to a particular group of persons being 'endangered' by the conduct (eg *Kennedy v Young* (1854) 1 Irv 533). In an appropriate case, this would amount to a simple, objective assessment of the conduct in relation to the circumstances; but it is not clear whether this is to be taken as a sufficient result, or indeed as a result at all.

Distress

3.08 'Distress' (caused to named individuals) was one of the specific results libelled in *Turner v Kennedy* ((1972) SCCR Supp 30), and in the burgh court a finding was made that some of these individuals had been 'distressed'. Findings of 'alarm', 'annoyance', and 'concern' were also made, however, which suggests that 'distress' might be insufficient *per se*. No guidance was given on the meaning of that term, but it may be that it is a psychological feeling appropriate to individuals rather than the lieges in general.

Disturbance

3.09 As 'disturbance' is traditionally associated with breach of the peace (see, for example, **1.03**, above), it is not surprising that this should be a commonly encountered result. It is rare, however, to find it expressly stated by itself in a charge (cf *Wright v Dewar* (1874) 2 Coup 504). Usually, if expressed at all, it will be found in combination with other recognised results (eg a minister and congregation were said to be 'disturbed and annoyed' in *Dougall v Dykes* (1861) 4 Irv 101; the lieges were said to be 'disturbed and annoyed' in *Allan v Lamb* (1900) 3 Adam 248; and, a religious meeting was said to be 'interrupted and disturbed' in *Hendry v Ferguson* (1883) 5 Coup 278). Nineteenth century charges where the essential consequence of the conduct was 'disturbance', were often colourfully elaborate (eg in *Hugh Fraser* (1839) 2 Swin 436, certain unseemly conduct in a church, charged as a breach of the public peace, was said to be to the great disturbance and disquietude of the congregation, the interruption of communion, the grievous outrage of the congregation's religious feelings, and the great scandal of all pious persons), but this is very far from being current practice. Today, it is more likely that one of the standard, simple styles (see **2.02**, above) will be employed and that the court will find (if appropriate) that disturbance was an actual or reasonably likely result. In *Robertson v Maxwell* (1951 SLT 46), for example, on a standard 'conduct yourself in a disorderly manner and

commit a breach of the peace' complaint, 'disturbance' was easily
found from the fact that the accused had knocked on doors of houses,
sung, and beaten upon an oil drum — all at 1 am on a Sunday.

Embarrassment

3.10   In *Sinclair v Annan* (1980 SLT (Notes) 55; 44 (1980) JCL 94), a
conviction for breach of the peace resulted from indecent remarks
made to two women. In the sheriff court there was no specific finding
of alarm or annoyance, but the sheriff did find that one of the women
had been 'embarrassed'. On a subsequent unsuccessful appeal based
on the ground that 'embarrassement' caused to one person was insufficient, the High Court affirmed that the sheriff had correctly
addressed himself to *Young v Heatly* (1959 JC 66 — see **2.41**, above)
and continued: 'It was open to him in the circumstances disclosed in
the findings to reach the conclusion that he did. The remarks in the
context in which they were uttered were of a particularly offensive
character and there is an express finding of embarrassment on the part
of Miss Mackay. In our judgment that was enough, if the sheriff so
chose to deal with it, to justify the conclusion that all the necessary
ingredients of the offence of breach of the peace had been made out.'
All that can be said here — given that the two reports of this case
neither specify the circumstances nor the nature of what was said — is
that the Appeal Court considered the 'embarrassment' of a particular
individual as a significant though not necessarily crucial issue. It is
possible that the circumstances were such that persons could have
reasonably been expected to be within the *locus*, and that any reasonable person would have been alarmed or annoyed by what had been
said. It is possible also that the case was properly one of 'shameless
indecency' (see *Watt v Annan* 1978 JC 84). But the reports only lend
themselves to conjectures. There was no discussion of what embarrassment should mean, nor whether it could be suffered by the lieges
(as opposed to individuals). The concept of the 'police offence' (see
1.17 ff, above) seems well to the fore here.

Fear

3.11   As 'alarm' seems to be thought of in terms of 'fear' of various
kinds (see **3.03**, above), it is difficult to distinguish the two, and thus
probably no distinction ought to be made. If this is so (and the OED
suggests that it is — s.v. 'alarm' and 'fear'), then charges which
specify both 'fear' and 'alarm' (eg *Raffaelli v Heatly* 1949 JC 101;

McLean v McNaughton 1984 SCCR 319; *Taylor v Hamilton* 1984 SCCR 393; *Benson v Tudhope* 1986 SCCR 422) are merely exercises in tautology (or emphasis). As pleonasm, however, has always been common in Scottish criminal charges, such a conclusion should occasion no surprise.

Obstruction

3.12 Several reported cases appear to include 'obstruction' as a result of conduct in charges of breach of the peace. The 'obstruction' referred to may be relative to the proceedings of a meeting (eg *Sleigh & Russell v Moxey* (1850) J Shaw 369) or to the flow of traffic (eg *Docherty v Thaw* (January 1962, unreported) High Court — see *Gordon* 41-04, fn 4) or to the free passage of the public (eg *Stirling v Herron* 1976 SLT (Notes) 2, and *Montgomery v Herron* (1976) SCCR Supp 131, where the complaint styles were identical). It is thought, however, that the 'obstructions' libelled in these cases were not true results as understood in relation to breach of the peace. Rather they were simply libelled as part of the *res gestae* which might give rise to a prescribed result. A meeting may be obstructed, for example, by legitimate police activity, and the obstruction of traffic may be achieved for desirable and lawful reasons. It is surely only where 'obstruction' can be said to be commensurate with (say) reasonable annoyance or alarm that breach of the peace can begin to be considered.

Outrage

3.13 'Outrage to religious feelings' was specified in at least one nineteenth century case, where there had been conduct which caused disturbance in a kirk (*Hugh Fraser* (1839) 2 Swin 436). This was merely an instance, it is thought, of the superfluity of expression common in pre-1887 indictments (and indeed it was also stated in *Hugh Fraser* that the conduct had been to the 'great scandal of all pious persons'). 'Outrage' in any event may simply be a higher form of 'annoyance'; and 'annoyance' combined with the undoubted 'disturbance' in the case would certainly have been sufficient.

Shock

3.14 Whether 'shock' or being 'shaken' is a sufficient result has never been tested. As it seems unlikely that one can envisage the lieges in general being 'shocked' or 'shaken', then if one or other of these is a relevant result *quoad* breach of the peace, the conduct will have to be the sort which has a victim — ie which is aimed at a specific person or at specific persons. This was the factual situation in *Hay v Wither* (1988 SCCR 334). There the accused on two separate occasions made homosexual advances to particular boys, and at his trial in the sheriff court for breach of the peace, it was found as a matter of fact that one of the boys was 'shaken' and the other 'shocked'. The adequacy of these findings for the purposes of the offence was not discussed on appeal (which was concerned with whether the principle derived from *Moorov v HM Advocate* (1930 JC 68) might be applied). But given the type of conduct complained of, and that it took place in a public toilet (in a public park) in one instance and in a public park in the other, there would have been little difficultly in inferring 'annoyance' or 'alarm' on the part of reasonable persons. The 'additional' finding of (say) 'shock' would probably have been unnecessary apart from its value in confirming the reasonableness of the inference which could be drawn and thus the reasonableness of the over-all conviction. This, however, is something of an *ex post facto* justification for the decision; but the case provides no real basis for considering 'shock' to be an adequate result on its own.

Temptation to make reprisals

3.15 If the conduct of the accused can be regarded as provocative to the point that others may reasonably be tempted to take violent and immediate action against its author (or his property or followers) then that temptation is apparently acceptable as a sufficient result for the purposes of breach of the peace. Lord Justice-Clerk Thomson (in *Raffaelli v Heatly* 1949 JC 101 at 104) is usually credited with the introduction of this as a live issue in that he said: '[W]here something is done in breach of public order or decorum which might reasonably be expected to lead to the lieges being . . . tempted to make reprisals at their own hand, the circumstances are such as to amount to a breach of the peace.' Although these words amounted to an *obiter dictum* in that case (where there was in fact evidence of alarm on the part of eye-witnesses — contrary to the view usually taken by commentators), they have been accepted (see **2.20**, above) as expressing a true element of the offence, to the extent that in *Wilson v Brown* (1982 SCCR 49) Lord Dunpark was able to state (at 51): 'It is well settled that a test which may be applied in charges of breach of the peace is whether the proved conduct may reasonably be expected . . . to provoke a disturbance of the peace.' If anything, this proceeds even further than Lord

Justice-Clerk Thomson's 'temptation to make reprisals' by broadening the matter beyond action taken against the author of the provocative conduct. What it does in fact is conflate the 'temptation to make reprisals' issue with that of 'conduct likely to occasion a breach of the peace'. It is thought, however, that Lord Dunpark's account points correctly to the true underlying issue — viz. — that what was done should reasonably provoke (or be capable of provoking) others to acts of minor violence, damage or the like, which can generally be described as 'a disturbance of the standing peace of the *locus*'.

3.16 If the above view is accepted, then it can be seen that Lord Justice-Clerk Thomson was expressing no novelty in *Raffaelli v Heatly*. For example, as far back as 1861, Lord Ardmillan (in *Dougall v Dykes* (1861) 4 Irv 101 at 105) said this: 'If any officer of the church should remove a man who was disturbing the order necessary in a place of worship, there can be no doubt that he would be supported by the law; and if a man's conduct be such as would warrant his removal on account of it, that conduct is clearly a breach of the peace.' In the same case, his colleague, Lord Neaves, was clearly of the same opinion when he stated (at 105–6): 'The conduct described was not only an insult to the minister, but also to the congregation, and was calculated to give rise to great irritation, and to a determination to repress it. It could not have been allowed to go on day after day, and the result would have been that some members of the congregation would have interfered to put a stop to it by force, and scenes of the most unseemly and violent nature might have been the consequence.' It seems then that conduct which reasonably provokes (or is capable of provoking) others to acts of minor violence or damage, has been sufficient for breach of the peace over many decades. It is also clear that the reprisals taken (or anticipated) *need not* themselves amount to breaches of the peace, or indeed any crime at all, on the part of those provoked (cf, for example, the situation in *Butcher v Jessop* 1989 SCCR 119). It seems a recipe for confusion, therefore, to address this sort of issue only in terms of 'conduct likely to occasion a breach of the peace'. That expression is not only odd in appearance (and unhelpful — viz. that a breach of the peace can be 'occasioned' by conduct which itself occasions a breach of the peace) but also fails to reflect the width of what is involved. (It is a matter for regret, therefore, that some charges of breach of the peace have been so expressed — see, for example, *Duffield v Skeen* 1981 SCCR 66, where the accused were charged that they did conduct themselves 'in a disorderly manner, shout inflammatory slogans likely to occasion a breach of the peace, and did thereby commit a breach of the peace'. What was meant, of course, in *Duffield* was that the accused's conduct might reasonably have led to a disturbance of some sort and not, surely, that those taking (or likely to take) action against them would necessarily have been unjustified in so doing and thus themselves guilty of the crime of breach of the peace. (Of course such persons *may* be guilty of breaches of the peace; but no such finding is necessary for the conviction of their provokers. See for example, *McAvoy v Jessop* 1989 SCCR 301.) The expression 'breach of the peace' is really there being used in two different senses — one legal (*qua* offence) and the other popular (ie as a synonymous expression for 'disturbance of the standing peace of the *locus*').

Terror

3.17   In nineteenth century charges of breach of the peace, it is sometimes said that what was done was such 'as to terrify and alarm' (eg, see *Macbeath v Fraser* (1886) 1 White 286) or was 'to the great annoyance, terror and alarm of the lieges' (eg, see *MacDougall v Maclullich* (1887) 1 White 328). 'Terror', being an advanced state of 'alarm' or 'fear', ought certainly to be a sufficient result for breach of the peace. But its use is now rare outside charges of mobbing and rioting (see eg, *Hancock v HM Advocate* 1981 SCCR 32). Indeed, *quoad* mobbing, words of the order 'to the great terror and alarm of the lieges' were stylistically required in nineteenth century charges — and still seem to be thought of as desirable today, notwithstanding the short forms introduced by the Criminal Procedure (Scotland) Act 1887 (Schedule A). In any event, breach of the peace cases (from last century) which included 'terror' as a result were invariably mobbing cases in all but name (see the full indictments, for example, in *Macbeath v Fraser* and *MacDougall v Maclullich*).

Upset

3.18   In *Raffaelli v Heatly* (1949 JC 101 at 104), Lord Justice-Clerk Thomson made apparent provision for 'upset' as a separate result in relation to breach of the peace, viz. '. . . [W]here something is done in breach of public order or decorum which might reasonably be expected to lead to the lieges being . . . upset . . ., the circumstances are such as to amount to breach of the peace'. This he distinguished from 'alarm' or 'temptation to make reprisals', but gave no guidance as to its meaning. It may be that he had 'annoyance' in mind; but, if so, that is not in accordance with later pronouncements on the general nature of the crime. Lord Dunpark, for example, in a much followed general statement, put the matter thus: '. . . [A] test which may be applied in a charge of breach of the peace is whether the proved conduct may reasonably be expected to cause any person to be alarmed, upset or annoyed or to provoke a disturbance of the peace' (*Wilson v Brown* 1982 SCCR 49 at 51). It remains for consideration, however, what 'upset' means in this context and whether 'upset' is a sufficient result on its own. In *McGivern v Jessop* (1988 SCCR 511), where a group of some twenty youths shouted insults and obscenities at Celtic Football-club supporters, the sheriff found as a fact that those supporters were 'quite upset'. (He also found, however, that a serious 'incident' — ie disturbance — was in the offing, and might well have occurred had the conduct been allowed to continue.) The later appeal against conviction in that case was abandoned. It may be that on a scale of values, 'upset' comes above 'embarrassment' and below 'annoyance' or 'alarm'; it may even be synonymous with a mental feeling of 'shock'. But nothing seems to have been settled here.

General

3.19 Consultation of the OED (1933 edn) for assistance with the meaning of the words considered above suggests that terror, alarm and fear may form one class of psychological feelings, whilst annoyance, shock, concern, distress, embarrassment and upset may form another. Further, the members of the former class may be characterised as mental, anticipatory reactions to dangers which are or seem imminent, whereas the latter class may be composed of psychological reactions to what has already happened. If such class arrangements were to be accepted, and the distinction between those classes kept in mind, it may be that less confusing complaints (and judgments) would be the beneficial results.

Conduct

General

3.20 Since a very wide variety of conduct has been considered sufficient (or, more accurately, has not been objected to) in breach of the peace cases, it is difficult to know what can be said in a general way relative to this aspect of the offence. Conduct on the part of the accused there clearly must be; but perhaps of greater importance are the circumstances in which it takes place (see, in particular, **2.51** to **2.69**, above). It is generally the circumstances which are crucial in determining whether one or other of the required results (see **3.01** to

3.19, above) was reasonably established or could reasonably be inferred. Nevertheless, conduct can, it is thought, be dealt with under particular heads — viz. 'assaults' (including violence generally), crowd action (including mobbing and rioting), sexual misconduct, verbal abuse, and unusual cases.

Assaults and other violent acts

3.21 In *Johnstone v Lindsay* ((1906) 5 Adam 192 at 195), Lord Justice-Clerk Macdonald took exception to a complaint which charged both assault and breach of the peace, on the basis that there was really only one incident and 'assault is a breach of the peace'. This does not mean, of course, that on a charge of breach of the peace, it is competent to convict of assault, or even to make a finding in fact that there was an assault (see *Butcher v Jessop* 1989 SCCR 119). What it does draw attention to is the very great difficulty in distinguishing between assault and breach of the peace where there has been an incident involving personal violence (see *Kennedy v Young* (1854) 1 Irv 533 at 539, per Lord Justice-Clerk Hope; *Butcher v Jessop*, per Lord Justice-Clerk Ross at p 131D–E). Prior to the recognition that consensual fighting was just a series of assaults (see *Smart v HM Advocate* 1975 JC 30), it might have been possible to make a distinction in terms of whether there had been agreement (even if tacit) to fight or not (a distinction which, incidentally, the prosecution in *Butcher v Jessop* still considered to have some validity). But, at present, it seems that the Crown may choose whichever offence they think more appropriate. If the incident, albeit lasting for a very short time, can be divided into a series of incidents, then this may be done — sometimes with evidential advantages for the prosecution (eg, see *McGinley v Macleod* 1963 SLT 2). A true assault, of course, should involve an 'attack on the person of another' (*Macdonald*, p 115) and an evil intent to injure or do bodily harm (as decided in *Smart v HM Advocate*). Presumably, if either of these cannot be shown, then a charge of breach of the peace would be the course of choice. But that may make it more difficult for the 'victim' to obtain civil damages (cf *Ross v Bryce* 1972 SLT (Sh Ct) 76) or compensation under the new criminal injuries compensation scheme (see the Criminal Justice Act 1988, s 109). It is not impossible for both assault and breach of the peace to be charged cumulatively in respect of the same incident; but it would then be a question of fact whether a conviction for both could be returned (cf *Scott v Stevenson* (1865) 5 Irv 86).

3.22   The brandishing of weapons (or household items pressed into service as such) has often featured as part of the narrative of a breach of the peace charge (eg *MacNeill v Robertson* 1982 SCCR 468 — sticks, bars and broken bottles; *Tudhope v O'Neill* 1983 SCCR 443 — sticks, a golf-club, umbrella shafts and plastic tubing). Once again, however, brandishing a weapon can be an assault (eg, see *Bryson v HMA* 1961 SLT 289 — brandishing a candlestick at a police officer and threatening to strike him with it), and it is thought that the point of distinction concerns whether or not the weapon was brandished at a particular person. If it was, the charge ought to be one of assault. *A fortiori*, discharging a firearm in a random way (eg into the air) is, if anything, a breach of the peace rather than an assault (eg, see *Palazzo v Copeland* 1976 JC 52), although it may also amount to a 'culpable and reckless' type crime, depending upon the facts (eg, see *Gizzi v Tudhope* 1982 SCCR 442).

3.23   Fighting and brawling are traditionally marked out as strong contenders for breach of the peace charges (see **1.05 ff**, above), wherever such conduct occurs (eg in a field, *Rodgers v Henderson* (1892) 3 White 151; in a street, *Wright v Dewar* (1874) 2 Coup 504; in a house, *Matthews & Rodden v Linton* (1860) 3 Irv 570; and, in a train compartment, *Hackston v Millar* (1906) 5 Adam 37). A challenge to fight is also sufficient; and it is now clear that such a challenge, actual scuffles and fighting, and violent acts in general may be proved on a complaint which specifies only 'disorderly conduct' (*Boyle v Wilson* 1988 SCCR 485; *Butcher v Jessop* 1989 SCCR 119). ('Disorderly conduct' is not, of course, confined to such aggressive acts — cf *Campbell v Adair* 1945 SLT 135). If a duel were to be fought today, or a challenge to participate in one were to be issued, such conduct would no doubt still be regarded as a very serious breach of the peace (see *James Bower Burns* (1842) 1 Broun 1, where the accused pled guilty).

3.24   *Hume* considered verbal threats to be breaches of the peace if they were 'violent and pointed' (see **1.12**, above), and this remains true (eg, see *Avery v Hilson* (1906) 5 Adam 56 — threat to shoot his wife with a gun which he had in his hand at the time; *Carey v Tudhope* 1984 SCCR 157 — general threats of violence to a particular person). But if the threats pertain to really serious injury, a separate offence of 'criminal threats' is now likely to be charged (eg, see *Kenny v HM Advocate* 1951 SLT 363 at 364, per opinion of Lord Keith; cf *Darroch v HM Advocate* 1980 SLT 33, where the charge was one of attempting to pervert the course of justice by means of verbal threats made over the phone).

Crowds

3.25   It has been held on several occasions that it is not a breach of the peace merely to gather a crowd around one, even if that was one's intention and even if the presence of that crowd was to the annoyance of some members of the public (*Marr v M'Arthur* (1878) 4 Coup 53 at 62, per Lord Adam; *Hutton v Main* (1891) 3 White 41 at 45, per Lord Justice-Clerk Macdonald). In one case (*Hutton v Main*), for example, a street preacher gathered a considerable crowd (600 to 700 strong) by singing and praying loudly for about half an hour. Some residents in the locality were annoyed by the noise (having been forced to close their windows against it); but Lord Justice-Clerk Macdonald (at 45) held that that was insufficient for breach of the peace unless the crowd could be shown to be disorderly or obstructive, or otherwise ought to have been dispersed. Although no guidance was given as to when a crowd would be considered disorderly or obstructive or should be dispersed, in the later case of *Whitchurch v Millar* ((1895) 2 Adam 9), the same judge (at 12) declared that he had no doubt that there had been a small, but relevant breach of the peace. There, Salvation Army personnel had marched vigorously and noisily through the streets of Hamilton at the head of a crowd of 30 to 40 persons. It was specifically libelled that the march had been disorderly, and it was found that the noise had been heard at a considerable distance from the location of the procession itself, as also that the crush of people had made it difficult for the lieges to pass through the streets. (An earlier case involving Salvationists had resulted in a similar conviction — see *Deakin v Milne* (1882) 5 Coup 174, but there, disturbance and actual fighting had been the results of similar prior marches through the Burgh of Arbroath.) It is not easy to see the fine distinctions which were obviously made in some of these cases, save that perhaps Salvation Army processions, being unorthodox and novel in the late nineteenth century, might more readily have been treated as public nuisances than conventional religious events. In any case, it has become customary to allege in relevant charges that a crowd had been 'disorderly'.

3.26   Genuine members of a disorderly crowd can each be convicted of breach of the peace, provided they have been appropriately charged. A competent (and minimalist) complaint might read as follows: 'You did form part of a disorderly crowd, shout and swear and commit a breach of the peace' (see *Muldoon v Herron* 1970 SLT 228). If the accused can be shown to have themselves shouted and sworn, there is, of course, no difficulty in obtaining a conviction (all other things being equal) — and, indeed, the reference to the crowd is probably superfluous. It is not necessary, however, to show that particular accused themselves shouted or swore (or whatever) (see *Montgomery v Herron* (1976) SCCR Supp 131; *Tudhope v O'Neill* 1983 SCCR 443) as long as they can be identified as having been in a relevant, disorderly crowd, and can also be shown to have been parties to some common plan (eg involving shouting and swearing) that that crowd was pursuing (*MacNeill v Robertson* 1982 SCCR 468 at 470, per Sheriff Scott). They would then be art and part guilty of breach of the peace. Reference to a 'common plan' is reminiscent of the 'common purpose' which mobbing and rioting requires (see **1.08**, above), and it may be thought that this will produce undesirable confusion between the 'separate' crimes of mobbing on the one hand and breach of the peace on the other. But it should be remembered that the distinction between these two offences is simply one of degree where crowds are involved (see **1.07** ff, above). Mobbing is simply a very serious form of mass breach of the peace.

3.27 Crowd behaviour which has been considered sufficient for breach of the peace has included forcible entry to a farm and woods (*Macbeath v Fraser* (1886) 1 White 286), mass shouting and swearing (eg *Bradford v McLeod* 1985 SCCR 379), stopping a horse-drawn vehicle and throwing stones and mud at its occupants (*MacDougall v Maclullich* (1887) 1 White 328), entering a school by force and causing damage there (*Bewglass v Blair* (1888) 1 White 574), rampaging throught the streets and shouting gang slogans (*Muldoon v Herron* 1970 SLT 228; *Tudhope v O'Neill* 1983 SCCR 443), tearing down a boundary wall and using the stones as missiles (*Winnik v Allan* 1986 SCCR 35), deliberately (note) obstructing the footpath to prevent a meeting taking place (*Stirling v Herron* 1976 SLT (Notes) 2), jostling the police (*Tudhope v Morrison* 1983 SCCR 262), forcing a way through a police cordon (*Tait v Allan* 1984 SCCR 385), and, making rude gestures to others (*Smith v Paterson* 1982 SCCR 295). Some of these cases, involved what is commonly called 'industrial action', and in one of them (*Tait v Allan* — where a miners' strike was involved) it was opined that a discount in sentence might normally be allowed for what was done in the heat of a bitter industrial dispute (although in the case itself the accused had no advantage of such a discount since it was entirely off-set by his long criminal record and by the fact that he was not an official picket).

3.28 *Quoad* mobbing and rioting, there must always be a common purpose (*Hancock v HM Advocate* 1981 SCCR 32). But it is difficult to see that such purpose plays a role which is radically different from that of the common plan necessary for art and part guilt of 'crowd' breach of the peace. It may be that 'common purposes' are expected to be of greater sophistication or intensity than 'common plans'; but the distinction, if it really exists, must be a fine one. For example, the following have proved acceptable purposes for mobbing: the prevention of collection of tolls (*McDonald v Mackay* (1842) 1 Broun 435); the rescuing of prisoners and deforcing of officers of law (*John Harper* (1842) 1 Broun 441); the intimidation of those still working during an industrial dispute (*John Duncan* (1843) 1 Broun 512; *Sloan v Macmillan* (1921) 2 SLT 296); the prevention of a ship from leaving harbour (*James Falconer* (1847) Arkley 242); the violent pursuance of sectarian rivalries (*Michael Hart* (1854) 1 Irv 574; *Robert McEwan* (1855) 2 Irv 217); and the forcible prevention of a summons being served (*Peter & Ann Ross* (1854) 1 Irv 540). As with a 'common plan', it is not necessary to reveal in a criminal charge what the precise 'purpose' was (see the Criminal Procedure (Scotland) Act 1887, Sch A, style of charge for mobbing and rioting); it must, however, be able to be inferred from the facts and circumstances (cf *Hancock v HM Advocate*).

Sexual misconduct

3.29   In an article critical of the decision in *Watt v Annan* (1978 SLT 198), there appears the following: '[T]he crime of breach of the peace is available to strike at any untoward behaviour in public' (see G Maher, 'The Enforcement of Morals Continued', 1978 SLT (News) 251 at 253). With the exception of the restriction to 'in public', one can readily illustrate the truth of that statement. 'Kerb-crawling' by male motorists, for example, is certainly dealt with by charging breach of the peace (eg, see *Lauder v Heatly* (1962, unreported) High Court — see JSF, 'Breach of the Peace', 78 (1962) Sc Law Rev 73 at 75); so also is voyeurism — even of the mildest variety (eg, see *Raffaelli v Heatly* 1949 JC 101). The handing out of pamphlets which *inter alia* advocated sexual freedom for school children was likewise considered as a breach of the peace (*Turner v Kennedy* (1972) SCCR Supp 30). Indecent suggestions, whether of a heterosexual (*Benson v Tudhope* 1986 SCCR 422), perverted (*Anderson v HM Advocate* 1974 SLT 239) or homosexual nature (*Hay v Wither* 1988 SCCR 334) are similarly handled, provided they do not proceed to actual lewd, indecent and libidinous practices (cf *Jessop v D* 1986 SCCR 716) or any other, serious sexual offence. Indecent remarks or suggestions may also be considered for prosecution as breaches of the peace (eg, see *Young v Heatly* 1959 JC 66).

3.30 Although few would disagree that sexually offensive conduct ought to be dealt with by the criminal law, there has been criticism of the use of breach of the peace for that purpose. The point made, which seems a valid one, is that a bald prior conviction for 'breach of the peace' (with its popular association with mere drunken brawling) may conceal the fact that the person concerned has suspicious sexual tendencies — and may, for example, enable employment to be undertaken which is eminently unsuitable for such a person (eg janitor of a primary school). The solution here would seem to consist in the enhancing of the recorded details of breach of the peace convictions so that concealment of the true crime is impossible. Thus 'breach of the peace — sexually molesting an 8-year-old female child' would be a highly desirable form of record in that situation.

Verbal abuse

3.31 Complaints for breach of the peace which specify that the accused 'bawled, shouted, cursed and swore' (eg, see *Marshall v MacDougall* 1986 SCCR 376) or 'shouted, swore and used obscene and abusive language' (eg, see *Carmichael v Boyle* 1985 SCCR 58) are extremely common. But what is meant by 'swearing'? Presumably, words of doubtful categorisation could be checked in a standard work (eg E Partridge *A Dictionary of Slang and Unconventional English* (5th edn, 1961)). There may be problems, however, in relation to foreign language expressions or even Americanisms. Nineteenth century case reports invariably spared their readers sight of the actual words which had been used; but modern reports are not nearly so coy. It can thus confidently be asserted that the following are current examples of swearing: 'There's the bastard I'm after' (*Marshall v MacDougall*); 'Aye, you fucking know Tam McGraw all right' (said by a policeman to a suspect — *Elliot v Tudhope* 1987 SCCR 85); 'Piss off; we're not moving for you cunts' (*Stewart v Jessop* 1988 SCCR 492); 'Fucking wankers' (*McGivern v Jessop* 1988 SCCR 511); 'Get the police bastards' (*Winnik v Allan* 1986 SCCR 35). It should be noted, however, that swearing has to be given out as such and intended as an insult to the addressee (see *Norris v McLeod* 1988 SCCR 572). If the swearing is in fact the simple (but coarse) everyday language used by persons of limited vocabulary, then it possibly does not qualify as conduct sufficient for breach of the peace (cf the expressions 'fuck off' and 'you cunts are always digging us up' as used by the accused in *Logan v Jessop* 1987 SCCR 604). The courts have also regarded it as highly significant that the accused refused to desist from swearing, or indeed from heaping abuse or insults on the victim's head (see, for example,

Norris v McLeod where the accused was warned about his language at least twice before being arrested).

3.32   When the language used as an insult to the recipient does not amount to conventional swearing, and particularly where it is not repeated, it appears that the courts will be loath to find that any crime has been committed. Thus, the expression 'you are a damned beast' was regarded as too trivial for even a local statutory offence in *Stirling v Murray* ((1883) 5 Coup 265); and an attempt to prosecute on account of opprobrious epithets applied to an inspector, and assistant inspector, of markets was dismissed as 'too ludicrous even to be analyzed' (*Buist v Linton* (1865) 5 Irv 210 at 213, per Lord Justice-Clerk Inglis; see also *Thomas Galbraith & William Muirhead* (1856) 2 Irv 520). Much will depend, however, upon what was said and in what circumstances, since the language used will probably have to amount to 'disorderly conduct' unless threats are involved (see **2.02**, above, and *Butcher v Jessop* 1989 SCCR 119 at 134c, per Lord Murray (dissenting)). It would seem, then, that the general approach to insulting language is not significantly dissimilar to that taken by *Hume* (see **1.12**, above).

Unusual conduct

3.33   It is not uncommon to read suggestions that attempted suicide may be considered as a breach of the peace (see, for example, *Gordon*, 23-01, fn 2; N G 'Legal Aspects of Suicide', 1958 SLT (News) 141 at 143), and some unreported cases give some additional credibility to these (eg *John MacLean* (1979) The Scotsman, 30 October, Inverness Sh Ct, who threatened to jump from scaffolding at a height of 100 feet in the centre of Inverness; *Johnston v Hilary* 1989 GWD 19-799, where the accused went onto a railway line and threatened to commit suicide). The circumstances, however, would have to be dramatic and special, such that others would genuinely and reasonably be alarmed by the behaviour (cf setting oneself alight at 12 noon on a Saturday in Princes Street, Edinburgh, and cutting one's wrists in the privacy of one's own home). To argue that it is necessary to consider such attempts as breaches of the peace to enable the police to take the unfortunate man or woman into 'protective' custody seems unduly paternalistic and overbearing.

3.34   It has also been claimed that blasphemy has *de facto* ceased to be a crime at common law in Scotland, but that the Crown might use breach of the peace instead (see G Maher, 'Blasphemy in Scots Law', 1977 SLT (News) 257 at 260). But what was, or is, blasphemy? According to *Hume* (I, ch xxix, p 368 ff), who was founding partly on common law and partly on now repealed Scots statutes, it consisted of the denial of the being of God, his attributes or nature, or the uttering of impious or profane things against God or the authority of the Holy Scriptures. It is thought that in a secular age, such as the present, there is no room for treating such matters in any special way. Thus, in the case of *Paul Stirling* (1989) The Scotsman, 28 June, Greenock Sh Ct, the accused disrupted a Christmas church service by *inter alia* shouting when the minister was reading from the Bible — 'Did you get that out of the yellow pages?' Such remarks certainly question the value of the 'Holy Scriptures'; but the blasphemous nature of the remarks is not of great importance. *Quoad* breach of the peace, the matter is determined rather by asking whether the conduct in the circumstances was reasonably likely to alarm or annoy those present at the service, or even whether it was likely to tempt them to make reprisals; and the answers, of course, are obvious.

3.35 Unusual examples, where again alarm or annoyance (or both? — since initial alarm may give way to annoyance when the truth becomes known) may readily be inferred, include discharging a distress flare for no good reason other than one's own idle amusement (but which led to a mountain rescue team and a helicopter being called out in the actual case of *George Law* (1988) The Scotsman, 9 March, Stonehaven Sh Ct); 'doodling' on the blotter provided for customers at a bank, but sketching where the security cameras were and adding notes such as 'explosive substances here', 'telephone wires cut here' (*James White* (1978) The Scotsman, 7 March, Glasgow Sh Ct); and, standing in a roadway, brandishing a replica revolver and forcing motorists to take avoiding action — all in an attempt to stop drivers speeding through the village of Braco in Perthshire (*Robert Cameron* (1989) The Scotsman, 28 April, Perth Sh Ct).

3.36 Some unusual cases, however, seem very far from recognised definitions of breach of the peace. What is to be said, for example, of playing marbles in the street on a Sunday afternoon (*John Meekison & Tutor v Mackay* (1848) Arkley 503), which the High Court seemed to think was 'disorderly conduct' (although a suspension of the conviction was allowed on the basis that it had been oppressive to arrest and prosecute a 10-year-old boy for such)? or taking part, as a professional, in a properly organised boxing match according to the Queensberry Rules (*Dobbs & Macdonald v Neilson* (1899) 3 Adam 10, where assault and breach of the peace were charged without objection)? or a male person's walking around dressed in women's clothing (*Robert Fraser* (1978) The Scotsman, 23 March, Perth Sh Ct, where a plea of guilty to breach of the peace was entered)? or the headline 'Hellish Worry of Church Fires' in a provincial newspaper report of the proceedings at a presbytery meeting (which the local procurator fiscal considered to be a definite breach of the peace, until over-ruled by the Lord Advocate — see *The Scotsman* 15 and 18 December 1986)?

3.37   There are also decisions which can only be described as inconsistent. In *Fisher v Keane* (1981 JC 50), for example, a conviction for breach of the peace by sniffing glue in a place where it could be observed by passers-by was quashed on appeal. But, later in the not-dissimilar case of *Taylor v Hamilton* (1984 SCCR 393), the conviction was upheld. Could it have been that, in the intervening period, 'glue sniffing' had come to be recognised as a major social problem and thus taken more seriously? Again, in the case of *Robert Mathieson* ((1983) The Scotsman, 8 September, Perth Sh Ct), the accused was acquitted of a charge of breach of the peace. He was found to have publicly displayed a placard which read: 'Vote for sexy Nick Fairbairn — the perjurer's pal.' The sheriff who heard the case accepted that the act in question was one of harmless eccentricity, not calculated to cause a disturbance. But less than a year later, following further 'placard' incidents in which the same man accused Fairbairn, the local procurator fiscal, a police chief, and three sheriffs of being 'cowardly, perjury-abetting vermin', a conviction for breach of the peace was imposed after trial (*Robert Mathieson* (1984) The Scotsman, 6 July, Perth Sh Ct). Can the difference simply have been one of the degree or extent of the accused's venom?

Conclusion

3.38   At one time, in the nineteenth century in particular, it was thought that behaviour which some found offensive or insulting or to which the adverb 'disorderly' might be applied, was not a breach of the peace, but criminal in some lesser capacity — either vaguely as a 'police offence' (see **1.17** ff, above) or under the loose terminology of some local Act. 'Disorderly conduct' especially was thought a fit subject for the police courts and their insignificant penalties. Today, given that breaches of the peace and police offences have merged under one general title (and that local Police Acts have mostly been — and shortly will all be — repealed), it is highly desirable that the 'reasonableness' requirement found in definitions of breach of the peace should not be lost sight of, and that common sense should prevail. It should never be the case that breach of the peace should depend on the emotional reactions of one witness, unless it can also be shown that the proved reaction would have been shared by reasonable persons of ordinary sensibilities (see *Taylor v Hamilton* 1984 SCCR 393). Further, it is important that breach of the peace should not be seen as a way of overcoming perceived (or imagined) gaps in the existing, substantive criminal law. But regrettably, the crime has been allowed to extend itself to eccentric and trivial behaviour (which happens to be disapproved of by some persons — very often the police) and to become an almost limitless instrument of social control. It is difficult to ascribe blame to any single source for these undesirable developments. But it is thought that these extensions will hardly be constrained without the active co-operation of accused persons themselves and their agents. In short, too many are persuaded, or persuade themselves, that the charges against them are not worth disputing — even where those charges are of the most dubious colour. Flexibility is the proud banner under which Scots criminal law advances. That is undeniable, and indeed inevitable in a dynamic common law system. But pragmatism must be tempered by common sense; and nowhere is there a greater need for that than in relation to the crime of breach of the peace.

Appendix

Ferguson v Carnochan — Parallel texts of the judgments.

Lord Justice-Clerk Macdonald

2 White 278 at 280ff	16 R (J) 93 at 94 ff

My Lords, there are two questions in this case. The first is, whether this being a charge of breach of the peace, that offence could be committed in a private house? In my opinion we must follow the decision in the case of *Matthews and Rodden*, and hold that a breach of the peace may be committed in a private house. The decision seems to me to be not only binding but sound. The second question is whether the facts set forth in this case are such as to warrant the magistrates in inferring that a breach of the peace had been committed, and I am of opinion that the magistrates were entitled to come to that decision on the facts set [p 281] forth. Breach of the peace consists in such acts as will reasonably produce alarm in the minds of the lieges; not necessarily alarm in the sense of personal fear, but such alarm as causes them to believe that what is being done causes, or will cause, real disturbance of the community, and the breaking up of the peace of the neighbourhood. And I do not doubt that sober and reasonably minded people might be seriously annoyed by a disturbance such as is set

There are two points in this case. The first is, whether the offence charged having taken place in the accused's own premises can constitute a breach of the peace. That point is ruled by the case of *Matthews and Rodden*, which decides, and I think soundly, that a breach of the peace may be committed in a private house.

The second point is, whether the facts disclosed are such that a breach of the peace can be inferred from them. I am of opinion that they are. Breach of the peace consists in such acts as will reasonably produce alarm in the minds of the lieges, not necessarily alarm in the sense of personal fear, but alarm lest if what is going on is allowed to continue it will lead to the breaking up of the social peace. The words 'to the alarm of the lieges' in a charge of breach of the peace mean that what is alleged was likely to alarm ordinary people, and if continued might cause serious disturbance to the community. In this case what is found proved is that the appellant was making a noise and disturbance and using loud language within his premises at an early hour upon a Sunday morning. He was heard by two con-forth in this case, being continued, and that it was a disturbance of the public peace.

The facts that are found proved are that the appellant was loudly disputing, cursing and swearing in his own house at an early hour of Sunday morning. This continued for some time, and at a distance of thirty yards two constables on their beat hear what is being shouted, and that particular individuals are being cursed. Accordingly they enter the premises, and the appellant is subsequently charged.

I am of opinion that a person using bad language in such a loud and noisy manner at three in the morning in his own house does commit a breach of the peace, and that the magistrates had sufficient evidence before them to justify them in convicting the appellant.

This case is practically the same as the case of *Matthews and Rodden*, except that here there was no fighting. That, however, makes no difference. The appeal therefore will be dismissed.

stables. About an hour afterwards the constables being again near the premises heard it still continuing, and from a distance of thirty yards were able to hear specific shouts directed against a particular individual accompanied by imprecations. I am of opinion that if a person at three o'clock on a Sunday morning uses loud language and oaths and imprecations so as to be heard at a considerable distance in the street of a town, he commits a breach of the peace, and therefore that the magistrates had before them facts sufficient to justify them in finding the accused guilty. The facts in this case are almost identical with those in the case of *Matthews and Rodden*, with the exception that in that case there was fighting. But as fighting inside of a house can affect persons outside only in so far as it causes noise in the street, I take it that the case of *Matthews and Rodden* would have been held equally relevant without the allegation of fighting.

Lord McLaren

2 White 278 at 281 ff

16 R (J) 93 at 94 ff

The question in this case is whether the facts found are sufficient to justify the magistrates in convicting the appellant, and that involves the further question as to what are the elements of fact which constitute a breach of the peace.

The question is, whether the facts found to be proved support the conviction, and that involves the consideration of what elements of fact are necessary to constitute the crime of breach of the peace. The clearest case of breach of the peace consists in

The clearest case of a breach of the peace is the engaging in hostilities; a street fight for example, or a prize fight in a private place, for it makes no difference whether the fight is in a public place or in a private place, if the lieges are alarmed. The term peace is not used as the antithesis of war. Breach of the peace [p 282] means a breach of public order and decorum, causing disturbance and alarm to members of the public.

Mere inarticulate noises or cries, such as street cries, are not breaches of the peace. On the other hand, where there is brawling, and where offensive language is used, it is not necessary that those who hear it should be alarmed for their personal safety. It is enough if the conduct of those who are found brawling and using the offensive language is such as to excite reasonable apprehension that mischief may ensue to the persons who are misconducting themselves, or to others.

I am satisfied that the disturbance caused, and the language used by the appellant, and heard in the public streets of Stranraer, aggravated by the occurrence being at night, amounts to a disturbance of the public peace. The facts stated being sufficient to warrant the Magistrates in convicting the appellant, I agree with your Lordship that the appeal should be dismissed.

engaging in hostilities either in the street or in a private ground, for I agree that it makes no difference whether the offence be committed in a public or private place, provided the lieges be alarmed. But breach of the peace is not confined to acts of this description. Breach of the peace means breach of public order and decorum, accompanied always by the qualification that it is to the alarm and annoyance of the public. Articulate noises and cries not calculated to be offensive to anyone have been held not to amount to breach of the peace. On the other hand where the brawling is of such a kind as to be offensive and alarming, it is not necessary that those who hear it should be alarmed for themselves. It is enough that offensive language should be uttered [p 95] in a noisy and clamorous manner so as to cause reasonable apprehension in the minds of those who hear it that some mischief may result to the public peace [26 SLR 624 at 625 adds: '— that is, to other persons than themselves'].

I am quite satisfied that the language used here, heard in the public street in Stranraer, with the aggravation that it was used at night and accompanied by noisy conduct, was calculated to be particularly disturbing, and that facts have been proved sufficient to justify the Magistrates in convicting.

[Lord Rutherfurd-Clark simply concurred.]

Index

All references are to paragraph numbers